The Secret Side of This Reality

Beyond Manifestation. How to Align with the Hidden Side of Life

The Hidden Architecture

Copyright © 2025 The Hidden Architecture
All rights reserved.

ISBN: 979-8-89860-310-6

No part of this publication may be reproduced, stored in a retrieval system, or transmitted in any form or by any means—electronic, mechanical, photocopying, recording, or otherwise—without the prior written permission of the author or publisher. All rights reserved under international and Pan-American copyright conventions.

Legal Notice: This publication is intended for personal use only. You may not modify, distribute, sell, use, quote, or paraphrase any part of this book without explicit consent from the author or publisher.

Disclaimer: The information contained within this book is provided for educational and entertainment purposes only. The author and publisher have made every effort to ensure the accuracy and completeness of the information presented. However, no warranties of any kind are expressed or implied. This book does not constitute legal, financial, medical, or professional advice. Readers should consult qualified professionals before applying any of the information contained herein. By reading this book, the reader agrees that the author and publisher shall not be held liable for any damages, losses, or liabilities caused directly or indirectly by the use or misuse of the information contained in this book, including but not limited to errors, omissions, or inaccuracies.

Once you see the hidden side of reality, you can never go back to the ordinary world

Table of Contents

Introduction: Why Reality Feels Incomplete 7

Part I. Foundations of Hidden Reality 19
    Chapter 1: The Hidden Mechanics of Reality 21
    Chapter 2: The Forgotten Laws That Govern Reality 33
    Chapter 3: Identity and the Self You Broadcast 45

Part II. Inner Transformation 56
    Chapter 4: Mastering Emotional Frequency 58
    Chapter 5: The Subconscious Operating System 67
    Chapter 6: Removing Resistance and Hidden Blocks 76

Part III — Quantum Application 85
    Chapter 7: The Structure of Quantum Possibility 87
    Chapter 8: Aligning Desire With Purpose 96
    Chapter 9: Applying the Framework to Key Life Areas 105

Part IV. Embodiment and Integration 115
    Chapter 10: Daily Practices That Reshape Reality 117
    Chapter 11: Living Permanently in the "Secret Side" 127
    Conclusion: The New Map of Reality 136

Introduction: Why Reality Feels Incomplete

The Hidden Half You've Been Missing

Most people sense, at least faintly, that there is more to life than what they can see. They may not have a framework for it, but they notice subtle patterns: coincidences that feel orchestrated, intuitive nudges that later prove true, moments where reality seems to bend in unexpected ways. These glimpses are not accidents. They are windows into a deeper layer of existence that operates quietly beneath what we call normal life.

From early childhood, you were taught to interpret reality only through what is visible and measurable. School lessons focused on logic, facts, and cause-and-effect processes that could be demonstrated in the physical world. Cultural narratives reinforced this by rewarding rational thinking and dismissing anything that did not fit into accepted frameworks. Even well-meaning parents often encouraged children to "stop daydreaming" or "be realistic," unintentionally closing the door on the subtler dimensions of human experience. Over time, you learn to tune out anything that cannot be weighed or seen, even when your inner senses still whisper that something else is happening beneath the surface.

The result is a kind of split existence. On one hand, you navigate daily life, solving problems, working toward goals, and managing responsibilities. On the other, there is an undercurrent of longing, a quiet awareness that what you have been shown is incomplete. You feel it in moments of synchronicity, in gut instincts you cannot explain, in flashes of insight that arrive out of nowhere. These experiences hint that there is more to reality than the straightforward stories you have been told. Ignoring them often leads to frustration or stagnation, because the tools you were given for creating change only work on part of the puzzle.

Understanding this hidden half begins with seeing reality as layered. The physical world is one layer: concrete, observable, and bound by linear time. Beneath it is an energetic layer that responds not just to action, but to intention, belief, and emotional state. These two layers are not separate; they are intertwined. Your thoughts and emotions influence how you interpret events, which in turn shapes the actions you take and the opportunities you notice. At the same time, shifts in external circumstances affect your inner world, reinforcing or challenging the beliefs you hold about what is possible. This interplay is constantly at work, yet most people remain unaware of it. They try to change their lives by rearranging the surface — switching jobs, ending relationships, starting new routines — without addressing the internal patterns that generate those outcomes. When the same frustrations reappear, they assume it must be bad luck or personal inadequacy. In reality, the deeper architecture of their lives has not changed, so new circumstances eventually replicate old dynamics.

Modern science, though cautious in language, has begun to hint at what ancient traditions have taught for centuries. Quantum physics shows that the act of observation affects outcomes. Neuroscience reveals that the brain filters perception according to expectations and emotional states. Psychology demonstrates that unconscious beliefs silently direct most of our choices. Spiritual teachings describe these same principles in terms of energy, vibration, and alignment. Together they point to a single conclusion: reality is participatory. You are not merely observing life unfold around you; you are influencing it at every moment, whether you realize it or not.

Recognizing this shifts everything. Instead of seeing yourself as a victim of random events, you begin to see patterns. You notice how inner resistance mirrors external obstacles, how moments of clarity invite unexpected breakthroughs, and how recurring challenges point to unhealed aspects of the self. This awareness does not instantly solve every problem, but it provides a map for navigating life with far greater precision and purpose.

As this understanding deepens, the way you approach personal growth shifts from force to alignment. Instead of trying to control every external detail, you begin working with the underlying currents that shape those details. This requires honesty about your inner state. Many people convince themselves they are thinking positively while carrying unacknowledged fears and resentments beneath the surface. These hidden emotions broadcast just as strongly as conscious intentions, influencing outcomes in ways that seem mysterious until you learn to recognize the signals.

Exploring the hidden half of reality is not about bypassing difficulties or pretending challenges do not exist. It is about recognizing that every experience, pleasant or painful, contains information about your inner alignment. When life feels stuck, it is often a sign that beliefs or patterns need to be examined rather than ignored. This approach replaces self-blame with curiosity. Instead of asking, "Why is this happening to me?" you ask, "What is this reflecting back to me?" That single shift in perspective transforms obstacles into feedback and provides a path forward that surface-level problem solving could never reveal.

Once you begin working with this deeper layer, subtle changes often appear before major ones. You may notice that conversations feel lighter, that opportunities arise without the usual struggle, or that certain habits fall away naturally instead of through willpower alone. These small shifts are not insignificant; they are indicators that your inner blueprint is changing. Over time, consistent alignment compounds, creating visible transformations in your outer world. The process is less about instant results and more about building an enduring relationship with the forces that govern your experience.

This relationship demands presence. It is easy to get caught up in mental loops about the past or anxieties about the future, but those states obscure the subtler signals that guide you. Awareness of the hidden half requires slowing down enough to feel what is happening within you right now. That might mean noticing how your body responds to certain thoughts, observing where tension arises when you consider a decision, or recognizing which environments drain or energize you. These observations provide clues about alignment that no external analysis can offer.

Practical integration becomes essential here. Understanding the hidden half in theory is not enough; it must be lived. Simple practices like conscious breathing, journaling patterns, or pausing before major choices create space for insight to surface. These are not rigid rituals but opportunities to align your inner state before acting. Over time, this practice shifts you from reacting to life to participating in its unfolding with intention.

The power of this awareness lies in how it reframes control. Rather than chasing control over every outcome, you cultivate influence over the only thing you truly can: your own alignment. Ironically, this inward focus often brings greater external results than relentless effort ever could. When you operate from coherence instead of inner conflict, reality tends to reflect that harmony in ways that feel effortless yet profound.

What makes this perspective transformative is its simplicity. It does not require adopting complex philosophies or rejecting practical action. It simply asks that you recognize the interplay between inner and outer worlds and learn to work with it consciously. This is the missing map most people never receive — a map that reveals not only how to navigate challenges but how to uncover meaning and purpose within them.

By acknowledging and learning to navigate the hidden half of reality, you gain access to possibilities that were always present but previously unseen. The rest of this journey will equip you with the tools to explore that map in detail, teaching you how to identify the deeper currents shaping your life and how to consciously align with them. With that foundation, every goal, every relationship, and every challenge begins to look different — not because the world changes overnight, but because you are finally seeing the whole picture.

Why Traditional Manifestation Advice Fails

For years, manifestation has been presented as a simple formula: think about what you want, visualize it daily, and watch it appear in your life. Countless books, courses, and social media posts reduce the process to positive thinking, vision boards, and repeating affirmations in front of a mirror. While these methods can sometimes lead to small changes, many people quietly struggle with the gap between what they are promised and what they experience. They do the work, speak the affirmations, stay optimistic, yet their circumstances remain stubbornly unchanged. This gap is not due to laziness or lack of faith. It is because much of the popular advice about manifestation leaves out critical pieces of how reality actually works.

Traditional manifestation teachings often assume that thought alone is the creative force. They imply that imagining a desired outcome repeatedly is enough to magnetize it into existence. The unspoken suggestion is that if nothing changes, you must not be visualizing hard enough or believing deeply enough. This places an unnecessary burden on people who are already doing their best. It also ignores the deeper mechanics at play, such as emotional resonance, subconscious programming, and alignment between desire and identity. Without addressing these layers, no amount of surface-level positivity can create lasting results.

The most overlooked factor is the role of the subconscious mind. Studies in neuroscience show that much of human behavior is driven by unconscious patterns formed in childhood. These patterns influence what we believe is possible, what we feel we deserve, and even how we interpret opportunities. Traditional manifestation advice rarely acknowledges this. It focuses on conscious intention while ignoring the beliefs operating beneath awareness. When the subconscious is filled with scarcity, fear, or unworthiness, it resists new outcomes even as the conscious mind tries to attract them. This inner conflict explains why so many people feel like they are pushing against an invisible wall.

Another missing element is emotional congruence. Reality responds less to the words you speak than to the emotions you embody. Saying "I am wealthy" means little if your emotional state is rooted in anxiety about money. The frequency of fear overpowers the surface declaration of abundance. This is not mystical thinking but a reflection of how the nervous system influences perception and decision-making. When emotions are misaligned with stated desires, people unconsciously sabotage opportunities or fail to notice them altogether. Traditional manifestation methods rarely address this subtle but powerful dynamic.

Popular advice also tends to ignore the importance of aligned action. Many teachings imply that once you set an intention, the universe will deliver everything without effort. While there are moments where life surprises us, most meaningful changes arise from a combination of inner alignment and practical steps. Visualization can open doors, but you must still walk through them. This does not mean hustling endlessly or forcing outcomes; it means being receptive to intuitive nudges and following through when opportunities arise. Without this balance, manifestation becomes passive wishing rather than participatory creation.

These shortcomings create a cycle of disappointment. People try the recommended practices, fail to see results, and blame themselves for doing it wrong. Some give up on the concept entirely, concluding that manifestation is either fake or reserved for a lucky few. Others double down, repeating affirmations louder or creating bigger vision boards, only to meet the same frustration. The core issue is not the desire itself but the incomplete understanding of how reality responds to thought, emotion, and energy in concert.

Breaking out of this cycle requires a shift in how we understand manifestation. Instead of treating it as a mental trick or a shortcut to bypass life's challenges, it needs to be approached as a process of alignment between mind, body, and deeper consciousness. This means recognizing that your external results are not random but reflections of the internal patterns you hold. When you shift those patterns, the external world often reorganizes naturally, sometimes in ways you could not have planned with logic alone.

A crucial aspect of this shift is confronting beliefs rather than layering positivity on top of them. When people ignore their doubts and repeat affirmations that do not feel true, they create tension within themselves. The conscious mind says one thing, but the body and subconscious know another. This dissonance produces mixed signals, which often manifests as inconsistency: brief moments of progress followed by setbacks. Addressing these beliefs head-on is not about indulging negativity; it is about acknowledging where you truly stand so you can create change from an honest foundation.

Emotional regulation becomes just as important as belief work. Many traditional methods ask you to force happiness or enthusiasm, which can feel unnatural when life circumstances are challenging. In reality, sustainable alignment is built by gradually moving up the emotional scale, not by leaping to an extreme state you cannot maintain. Learning to soothe anxiety, cultivate gratitude in small ways, and find calm in the present moment builds a more stable energetic baseline. From this place, visualizations and intentions gain potency because they are no longer fighting against underlying turmoil.

Practical engagement with life completes the picture. Traditional manifestation advice often overcorrects from a culture of overwork by promising effortless results. While it is true that inspired opportunities arise when you are aligned, those opportunities still require action. A phone call must be made, a conversation must be had, a decision must be followed through. The difference is that action taken from alignment feels lighter and more guided, rather than frantic or forced. When both inner and outer worlds are addressed, manifestation ceases to be a passive hope and becomes a co-creative process.

This perspective also explains why results often appear in layers rather than all at once. Aligning with a new reality does not always produce an instant external transformation, but it sets a trajectory where the right people, insights, and resources converge over time. Each aligned choice builds momentum, gradually replacing old patterns with new ones until the shift becomes visible and undeniable. Seeing manifestation as an unfolding rather than an event helps sustain patience and commitment when immediate results are not obvious.

When these deeper elements are understood, the shortcomings of traditional advice become clear. The problem was never that visualization or affirmations were useless; it was that they were incomplete. They can be powerful tools when paired with belief work, emotional awareness, and aligned action. Without those components, they remain surface-level practices that often leave seekers disillusioned. With them, they become part of a holistic process that bridges the visible and invisible layers of reality.

This book is designed to provide that bridge. It does not dismiss the value of techniques people already know, but it places them within a framework that addresses the missing pieces. By the time you reach the later chapters, you will understand not just what to do, but why it works and how to apply it consistently. The aim is not temporary excitement but lasting transformation — the kind that changes not only what you experience but how you experience life itself.

A New Framework for Accessing Reality's Deeper Layers

Most people approach life as if it were a one-dimensional surface, believing that what they see, touch, and measure is all there is. When reality does not respond the way they hope, they either blame themselves or conclude that unseen forces are random and beyond comprehension. The truth is more nuanced. Reality has depth. Beneath the surface events you observe lies a network of influences that can be understood and engaged with, but only if you adopt a framework that accounts for both the seen and unseen aspects of life.

The purpose of this framework is to give you a practical way to navigate those deeper layers without losing clarity. It is not about adopting a rigid philosophy or discarding common sense. Instead, it integrates what ancient traditions have intuited for centuries with insights from modern psychology and physics. By seeing these layers together, you begin to understand why some efforts feel effortless while others feel like an uphill battle, and why certain people seem to flow toward opportunities while others stay locked in struggle despite equal effort.

At its core, this framework recognizes three interwoven dimensions: the physical, the psychological, and the energetic. The physical layer is the one you are most familiar with — actions, environments, and tangible outcomes. The psychological layer consists of beliefs, perceptions, and patterns shaped by your personal history. The energetic layer refers to the subtle frequencies created by your emotions, intentions, and state of being. Traditional approaches to success and change often address one of these dimensions in isolation. They might focus on behavior while ignoring belief, or emphasize positive thinking without grounding it in practical action. This fragmented approach leads to inconsistent results because the layers are inseparable. Change in one inevitably affects the others, and alignment across all three creates the conditions for transformation.

Understanding these dimensions begins with the recognition that your experience of life is filtered through perception. Two people can encounter the same event and interpret it in entirely different ways, shaping their subsequent actions and outcomes. This is why simply forcing positive thoughts is insufficient. If the deeper layers of perception remain unexamined, you will continue to interpret experiences through old filters that reinforce old realities. The framework invites you to uncover and rewrite those filters so your perception begins to align with what you truly want to create.

Equally important is the energetic layer, which is often misunderstood or oversimplified in popular teachings. Energy is not mystical in this context; it refers to the measurable ways your internal state influences behavior and relationships. People pick up on subtle cues — body language, tone, presence — often without conscious awareness. Opportunities and interactions unfold differently when you are calm and centered compared to when you are anxious or resentful. This is why emotional alignment matters as much as strategic action. The framework helps you cultivate an internal state that supports rather than sabotages your goals.

When these three dimensions are addressed together, a clearer path emerges. You stop chasing outcomes blindly and start noticing how reality responds to your internal shifts. Patterns that once felt random begin to reveal structure. You see how recurring challenges are invitations to realign rather than punishments to endure. This awareness does not eliminate difficulty, but it changes your relationship to it, transforming struggle into feedback and uncertainty into opportunity.

The next step is learning how to work with this framework deliberately rather than by chance. To do that, we begin by mapping out how these layers interact in everyday life and how you can consciously influence them without falling into the trap of forced positivity or blind control.

To work with this framework effectively, you must first become aware of which dimension is currently driving your experience. In moments of frustration, is the issue rooted in your external circumstances, in your internal beliefs, or in the emotional energy you carry? This level of self-inquiry prevents you from treating symptoms rather than causes. For example, if financial struggles persist despite taking practical steps, it is worth examining whether deeper beliefs about scarcity or unworthiness are influencing your choices and subtly guiding you away from opportunities. Addressing the underlying layer creates a shift that actions alone cannot achieve.

The interplay between these layers also reveals why sustainable change often feels gradual rather than instantaneous. As one layer begins to shift, the others follow. Aligning beliefs without taking corresponding action creates stagnation. Acting boldly while ignoring unresolved fears leads to self-sabotage. Regulating emotions without examining outdated perceptions results in temporary relief but little lasting growth. True alignment happens when your thoughts, emotions, and actions point in the same direction, forming a coherent signal that reality responds to more consistently.

Practical tools become more powerful when seen through this integrated lens. Visualization is no longer about daydreaming; it is a way of training perception to notice possibilities previously overlooked. Affirmations are not magic words but reminders that interrupt unconscious narratives and gradually install new ones. Mindfulness practices are not just stress reducers; they are gateways to observing the subtle shifts in energy that precede external change. When these tools are used with awareness of all three dimensions, they stop feeling like empty rituals and start functioning as catalysts for transformation.

This framework also provides a way to navigate challenges without losing momentum. Life will still present difficulties, but the meaning you assign to them changes. Obstacles become feedback rather than signs of failure. Emotional triggers become indicators of where alignment is needed rather than evidence of weakness. This perspective removes the false expectation that growth should feel effortless. Instead, it normalizes discomfort as part of the recalibration process, allowing you to stay engaged without slipping into discouragement.

Another benefit of working with these layers is the sense of agency it cultivates. Many people swing between extremes of control and helplessness — either trying to force outcomes through sheer effort or waiting passively for life to deliver miracles. The framework offers a middle path. It teaches you to take responsibility for your internal state and your actions without assuming you must micromanage every detail of the external world. This balance creates space for both discipline and trust, which are essential for navigating uncertainty.

Over time, engaging reality through this lens reshapes your entire orientation to life. You begin to anticipate patterns before they fully manifest, which allows for proactive rather than reactive choices. Relationships improve as you recognize the role your inner state plays in every interaction. Opportunities seem to appear more frequently, not because the world has changed, but because you have tuned into possibilities that were always present. This is the quiet power of alignment:

it transforms the way you participate in life rather than demanding that life conform to your will.

The chapters ahead will explore each dimension in greater depth and provide concrete practices for working with them. You will learn how to uncover subconscious beliefs, regulate emotional energy, and align actions with inner clarity. More importantly, you will see how these practices interlock into a cohesive system rather than scattered techniques. By the time you integrate these layers, you will have more than a set of tools — you will have a map for living in a way that feels both intentional and connected to the deeper currents of reality.

Part I. Foundations of Hidden Reality

Every meaningful journey begins with understanding where you are starting from and what has been missing up until now. For most people, the idea of shaping reality is not new. They have heard fragments of it through popular books, social media soundbites, or motivational speeches. They know the phrases about "positive thinking" and "visualizing success," and some have even tried them. Yet beneath that familiarity lies quiet frustration. The methods they were given often feel incomplete. Results come slowly, inconsistently, or not at all, leaving them wondering if the promise itself was flawed or if they were somehow doing it wrong.

The truth is neither. The promise that reality can be influenced from within is real, but the understanding most people receive is partial. It focuses on one piece of a much larger system, like being handed a single gear without being shown the rest of the clockwork. Without context, that gear seems useless. With the full picture, it becomes essential. The purpose of this part of the book is to reveal that larger system — the hidden foundations that determine why life unfolds the way it does and how you can begin to work with it rather than against it.

These foundations challenge the assumptions most of us were taught about what is "real." We have been conditioned to view life as linear and mechanical: events happen to us, and we respond. Success is earned by effort, and failure is proof of personal shortcomings. But this surface-level model leaves out a crucial dimension: the way your beliefs, emotions, and energy interact with reality itself. When you begin to account for this deeper layer, life stops looking random and starts revealing patterns. You see how your inner state influences your outer circumstances and how shifts in perception can lead to entirely different outcomes without changing a single external factor.

This is not about abandoning reason or retreating into mysticism. It is about expanding your map of reality so it finally matches what you have sensed all along — that there is more to life than what you can see, and that "more" is not chaos but an underlying structure waiting to be understood. Ancient spiritual traditions hinted at this structure in their own symbolic language. Modern science, though cautious, now echoes some of these insights through fields like quantum physics and neuroscience. When woven together, these perspectives form a coherent explanation for why your inner work matters and why ignoring it keeps you stuck in repetitive cycles.

Foundations matter because everything that follows is built on them. If you skip this understanding, later practices risk becoming hollow routines. Visualization becomes empty daydreaming rather than focused creation. Affirmations become words spoken without resonance. Even well-intentioned action becomes frantic effort disconnected from deeper alignment. By grounding yourself in these foundations first, every technique you learn later gains context and power.

As you enter this section, keep an open mind but also a discerning one. Some ideas may challenge what you have been taught about how life works. That is a good sign. The deeper layers of reality often defy surface expectations, yet they explain much of what you have intuitively felt but could not articulate. This part of the book will not ask you to accept anything blindly. It will invite you to test these concepts against your own experience and notice how life begins to respond differently when you approach it from this expanded perspective.

With these foundations in place, you will be prepared to explore the deeper mechanics of energy, frequency, and consciousness, and begin seeing the patterns that have been shaping your life all along.

Chapter 1: The Hidden Mechanics of Reality

Energy, Frequency, and Consciousness. The Real Building Blocks of Life

Everything you experience is shaped by forces that go beyond the physical matter you can touch. Beneath the world of solid objects and measurable events lies a more subtle reality made up of energy, frequency, and consciousness. These three elements interact constantly, creating the patterns you call life. Understanding them is not just an abstract concept. It is the foundation for learning how to work with reality rather than feeling like it is happening to you.

Modern science hints at this through discoveries in quantum physics. At the smallest levels of existence, particles are not fixed things but vibrating fields of energy. They respond to observation and shift according to context, behaving differently depending on how they are measured. This is not mystical speculation; it is documented scientific behavior. The implication is profound: the building blocks of everything you see, including your own body, are not static but fluid, influenced by conditions and interactions rather than fixed in place.

Frequency is another way of describing this vibrational nature. Every form of energy has a frequency — a rate at which it oscillates. In practical terms, this means that the thoughts you think and the emotions you feel also carry a frequency. These frequencies interact with your environment in ways that shape your perceptions and even the opportunities that seem to appear in your life. You may have noticed how being around someone joyful feels different from being around someone resentful, even if they say nothing. That difference is frequency at work.

Consciousness ties these elements together. It is the awareness that observes, directs, and interprets energy. Without consciousness, energy is neutral; it simply exists. Consciousness gives it meaning and intention. This is why two people can experience the same event yet respond completely differently — their consciousness interprets the energy through unique filters. Those filters, shaped by beliefs and experiences, determine whether they perceive an opportunity, a threat, or nothing significant at all.

When you begin to view reality through this lens, life stops appearing as a chain of random events. Instead, you see it as a dynamic interaction between your internal state and the field of possibilities around you. Energy responds to focus. Frequency shifts with emotional regulation. Consciousness directs where energy flows. This is not about controlling every detail of life but about learning to align these elements so that they work together rather than in conflict.

Many people misunderstand this interplay and think of energy work as detached from practical life. They imagine it as abstract or mystical, something separate from daily decisions. In truth, it is deeply practical. Every choice you make is influenced by your energy in that moment. When you are anxious, you interpret situations through a narrow lens and often miss opportunities. When you are grounded and centered, the same situations reveal options that were invisible before. This is why cultivating awareness of your energy and frequency is essential for meaningful change.

Developing this awareness begins with noticing patterns rather than trying to force outcomes. Pay attention to how certain thoughts create a physical response in your body, how your energy shifts in different environments, and how your emotions fluctuate throughout the day. These observations reveal the frequencies you are broadcasting, often unconsciously. Once you recognize them, you gain the ability to adjust them intentionally, which in turn influences the reality you experience.

This is not about perfection or never feeling negative emotions. It is about becoming skilled at recognizing when your frequency is misaligned and learning how to bring it back into harmony. That skill is what separates fleeting moments of clarity from a sustainable practice of living in alignment with the deeper mechanics of reality.

The moment you understand that energy and frequency are always active, you begin to see why certain habits and environments either support or sabotage growth. The people you spend time with, the spaces you inhabit, even the information you consume all carry their own energetic signatures. These influences subtly interact with your own state, often amplifying it. This is why surrounding yourself with chaos or negativity tends to perpetuate inner turmoil, while supportive environments seem to naturally lift you. Awareness of this interplay allows you to make deliberate choices rather than passively absorbing the energy around you.

Consciousness is the key factor that turns this knowledge into power. While energy flows and frequencies shift constantly, it is your awareness that determines whether you react unconsciously or engage intentionally. Consciousness lets you pause between stimulus and response, creating room to choose. In that space, you can redirect your focus, adjust your internal state, and influence how energy organizes around you. This subtle shift often produces changes that seem almost effortless, not because life suddenly became easy, but because your relationship with it changed.

Practical engagement with these principles begins with observation rather than control. Spend time noticing the connection between your inner state and the outcomes you experience. Do certain emotional patterns precede particular challenges? Do moments of clarity or peace coincide with opportunities appearing unexpectedly? This kind of tracking provides evidence that reinforces the reality of these dynamics. It also highlights where misalignments occur so they can be addressed at the root rather than on the surface.

Once you start observing these patterns, simple adjustments become powerful. Calming the body through breathing can shift frequency from fear to clarity. Reframing a limiting belief can free energy that was previously tied up in resistance. Taking inspired action at the right moment can amplify results because it aligns intention with opportunity. These shifts may appear small in the moment, but their cumulative effect transforms how life unfolds over time.

Working with these building blocks does not require withdrawing from the practical world or abandoning rational thought. In fact, it enhances your ability to navigate life's challenges. When you understand that external struggles often mirror internal imbalances, you gain new tools for problem-solving. Instead of only addressing symptoms, you look for the energetic and perceptual patterns creating them. This layered approach is what separates temporary relief from lasting transformation.

As you continue applying this framework, the boundaries between inner and outer reality begin to blur. Life feels less like a series of disconnected events and more like a dialogue between you and the larger field of possibilities. Synchronicities become more frequent, not as magical interventions, but as natural reflections of alignment. You stop chasing control over every outcome and start cultivating the internal coherence that naturally attracts what you need.

Mastering these elements is not about reaching a state of permanent perfection. It is about building resilience and flexibility so you can realign quickly when life inevitably throws challenges your way. With practice, energy, frequency, and consciousness become tools rather than mysteries. They provide a reliable foundation for everything else in this book, allowing you to engage the deeper layers of reality with clarity and purpose rather than guesswork or blind faith.

The Observer Effect: How Attention Shapes Experience

One of the most fascinating discoveries in modern physics is known as the observer effect. At its core, it reveals that the act of observing something can change what is being observed. In experiments at the quantum level, particles behave differently depending on whether they are being measured. They can exist in multiple potential states until attention is applied, at which point one possibility becomes actualized. While this principle was first identified in controlled scientific environments, its implications reach far beyond laboratories. It points toward a truth that ancient spiritual traditions have long suggested: your awareness is not passive. It actively participates in shaping the reality you experience.

This principle helps explain why two people can face the same external situation and walk away with entirely different experiences. Attention acts like a spotlight. Whatever you direct it toward becomes amplified in your perception and, over time, in your reality. If your focus rests constantly on what is lacking, that sense of lack grows stronger, influencing your choices and reinforcing the very circumstances you wish to escape. If your attention shifts toward possibilities and alignment, your decisions begin to reflect that new orientation, creating opportunities that once felt invisible.

The observer effect is not about magical thinking. It is about recognizing how perception and attention guide behavior and outcomes. Neuroscience confirms that the brain filters the world based on what it deems important. This filtering process, known as the reticular activating system, constantly scans your environment for information that matches your dominant focus. When you fixate on problems, you unconsciously train your mind to find more evidence of them. When you cultivate awareness of opportunities, your brain begins noticing resources and pathways that were previously overlooked.

This has profound implications for manifestation and personal transformation. Many people try to change their lives by force — pushing harder, working longer, striving to fix external conditions — without realizing that their attention is locked on what they are trying to avoid. Their focus is on lack, fear, or resistance, which unintentionally reinforces those states. Shifting attention does not mean ignoring challenges; it means observing them without letting them dominate your mental and emotional field. This subtle shift creates space for new patterns to emerge.

Developing skillful attention requires practice. Most people allow their focus to drift unconsciously, shaped by habits, social media, and constant external stimulation. The mind jumps between worries about the future and regrets about the past, rarely pausing in the present moment. This scattered attention weakens creative power. By contrast, deliberate attention anchors you. It enables you to respond thoughtfully rather than react automatically, and it directs your energy toward what you want to grow rather than what you fear.

Attention also influences emotional energy. Where focus goes, emotion follows. Dwelling on perceived threats fuels anxiety, while noticing small moments of gratitude begins to generate calm and openness. Over time, these emotional patterns create feedback loops that either limit or expand your possibilities. When you become aware of this loop, you gain the ability to interrupt it. Choosing where to place your focus becomes one of the most powerful levers for transforming your experience, because it shifts not only your perception but also your state of being.

Understanding this effect does not mean denying difficulty or pretending life is perfect. It means learning to observe without collapsing into judgment, to hold awareness of problems while also directing attention toward solutions. This balanced focus keeps you grounded while remaining open to new possibilities. It bridges the gap between spiritual insight and practical living, showing you that the power to shape reality lies not in controlling every outcome but in mastering where you place your awareness. Training your attention is less about learning something new and more about reclaiming a skill you have always had. You are already observing and interpreting constantly, but without conscious direction that process runs on autopilot, guided by old conditioning and unresolved fears. When you begin to take ownership of what you notice and how you respond, the world starts to shift in subtle but unmistakable ways. Small choices in focus ripple outward, influencing mood, decisions, and eventually outcomes.

One of the simplest ways to apply this is by becoming aware of your dominant questions. The human mind is naturally curious and seeks answers to whatever question is most active. If you constantly ask, "Why does nothing work out for me?" the mind will search for evidence to confirm that assumption. If you shift the question to, "What opportunities am I not noticing yet?" the same mind begins scanning for new possibilities.

The external world may not have changed in that moment, but your internal lens has, which means your behavior and receptivity will change with it.

Another important aspect is noticing how attention interacts with emotion. When you dwell on a thought long enough, it triggers a corresponding feeling, which then reinforces the thought in a loop. A single worry can grow into full-blown anxiety simply because it receives uninterrupted focus. By redirecting attention to something stabilizing — a breath, a grounding sensation, a constructive action — you disrupt the loop and create space for a different emotional state to emerge. Over time, this capacity to shift focus becomes one of your most powerful tools for emotional regulation and conscious creation.

This principle is not limited to internal experiences. It also affects how you engage with others. People often mirror the attention they receive. When you approach someone expecting conflict, subtle cues in your body language and tone may provoke defensiveness even if you say nothing overtly aggressive. Conversely, when you approach with openness and curiosity, you invite a different response. The interaction itself becomes a reflection of the attention you bring into it. Recognizing this helps you take responsibility for the energy you contribute to every relationship and situation.

The observer effect also explains why mindfulness and presence are emphasized in so many transformative practices. When you are fully present, your attention stops scattering across imagined futures or replayed past events. In that stillness, you gain clarity about what is actually happening and what needs to be done. Presence allows you to respond to life as it is rather than as your fears or expectations paint it. This shift is subtle but profound; it changes not just how you experience reality but how reality responds to you.

Mastering attention is not about perfection. There will be moments when your focus drifts to worry, doubt, or negativity. The key is not to judge yourself but to notice and gently return to alignment. Every time you make that return, you strengthen your capacity to direct your awareness intentionally. Over time, this becomes second nature, and you begin to live less as a passive participant and more as a conscious creator of your experience.

As you move forward in this book, this principle will become a recurring thread. The practices ahead — whether involving energy work, identity shifts, or emotional recalibration — all rely on your ability to notice where your attention is and to guide it where it serves you best. Without this, even the most powerful techniques lose effectiveness. With it, ordinary moments transform into opportunities for alignment, and life begins to feel less like chaos and more like a conversation you are finally able to participate in fully.

Distinguishing Illusion from Truth: Seeing Beyond the Surface

Much of what shapes human experience is not objective reality but the interpretations layered on top of it. Two people can live through the same event and tell two entirely different stories about what happened, each convinced theirs is the truth. This does not mean there is no reality. It means that most of what we call reality is filtered through perception — and perception is shaped by beliefs, memories, and conditioning. Learning to separate illusion from truth is essential for anyone seeking to work with the deeper mechanics of life, because without this skill, you may spend years trying to solve problems that exist only in your interpretation of events.

Illusion arises when perception becomes distorted, either by fear, desire, or unquestioned assumptions. For example, you may perceive rejection in someone's silence when in reality they are distracted or preoccupied. You might interpret a temporary setback as permanent failure because it mirrors an old wound. The mind creates meaning quickly, often without pausing to question whether that meaning is accurate. These distortions are not malicious; they are survival mechanisms. The brain evolved to predict danger and protect you, but that protective instinct often mistakes discomfort for threat, creating patterns of avoidance or defensiveness that do not serve you in modern life.

Truth, in contrast, is what remains when those distortions are stripped away. It is rarely as dramatic as the stories the mind tells. Truth tends to be simple and neutral: a fact about what is happening right now rather than a prediction about what it means for the future. Distinguishing truth from illusion requires slowing down and observing your own reactions. When you feel triggered, ask whether the intensity of your response is truly about the present moment or whether it echoes something older. Often, the mind overlays past pain onto current circumstances, convincing you that you are seeing clearly when in fact you are reacting to memory.

This process of discernment is not about dismissing emotions or pretending that everything is fine. Emotions are real signals and deserve attention. The key is to recognize that emotions do not always reveal objective truth; they reveal what feels true to you based on your current inner landscape. By understanding this, you can honor your feelings without letting them define reality. For example, feeling unsafe does not always mean you are unsafe. It may indicate a pattern of vigilance developed in response to earlier experiences. Recognizing this difference allows you to respond with wisdom instead of reflex.

Another layer of illusion comes from cultural and social conditioning. From childhood, you absorb narratives about success, love, worthiness, and security. These narratives shape what you strive for and how you judge yourself. Many people chase goals they do not truly value because they have inherited someone else's definition of fulfillment. They assume that wealth, status, or approval will bring happiness, only to find themselves empty once those milestones are reached. Peeling back these cultural illusions requires deep self-inquiry: asking whose values you are living by and whether those values align with what feels authentic to you.

The work of seeing beyond illusion does not mean discarding every belief or doubting everything you perceive. It means approaching your perceptions with curiosity rather than certainty. It means testing assumptions against lived experience and being willing to adjust when evidence reveals something new. This openness creates flexibility and reduces suffering, because much of human pain arises not from events themselves but from the rigid stories we attach to them. When you learn to hold your interpretations lightly, life becomes less threatening and more fluid.

A practical way to begin separating illusion from truth is to notice where your mind moves instantly to conclusions. When something happens, pay attention to the story you tell yourself about it. Do you assume someone's tone means disapproval? Do you interpret silence as rejection or judgment? Do you label an obstacle as a sign you are failing? Observing these automatic interpretations allows you to question them instead of accepting them as fact. Even a brief pause between the event and the story creates space for clarity.

This pause is not about suppressing thoughts but about stepping back enough to ask, "What is actually happening right now?" Often, the raw fact is neutral — an unanswered text, a missed opportunity, an unexpected comment. The suffering comes from the meaning added to it: "They must not care," "I am not good enough," "Nothing ever works out." By noticing the difference between the fact and the interpretation, you begin dismantling illusions that have shaped your reality for years.

Another aspect of this discernment is understanding how deeply emotions influence perception. When you are angry, everything feels unjust. When you are afraid, everything feels dangerous. These emotional states color your interpretation of events, making illusions seem real. Recognizing this does not mean dismissing emotions but balancing them with observation. Ask yourself whether the emotion reflects the present moment or whether it is magnifying a fear rooted in the past. This question helps prevent temporary feelings from becoming permanent conclusions.

Over time, this practice builds inner stability. You become less reactive to surface fluctuations because you no longer assume every perception is absolute truth. Challenges still arise, but they no longer carry the same power to destabilize you. By learning to see beyond illusion, you respond to life rather than react blindly to it. This shift is subtle yet transformative. It turns difficulties into opportunities for insight and prevents you from being pulled into cycles of unnecessary suffering.

Cultural narratives can be more difficult to spot because they are so pervasive. They often appear as unquestioned "shoulds": you should have achieved more by a certain age, you should look a certain way, you should want what everyone else wants. These inherited expectations create illusions about what success or happiness must look like. To uncover them, ask whether the goals you are pursuing genuinely resonate with you or whether they were handed down by family, peers, or society. Releasing illusions of this kind frees immense energy, allowing you to pursue what actually matters to you rather than what you think you are supposed to value.

When illusions fall away, what remains is a quieter kind of truth. It is not dramatic or loud. It is a calm recognition of what is real in this moment. This truth often feels lighter because it carries no extra story, no exaggerated prediction, no unnecessary weight. From this place, your choices become clearer. You stop reacting to imagined threats and start acting in alignment with what is actually happening. This clarity allows you to conserve energy and focus it where it will create meaningful change.

Living from this clarity does not mean you will never be influenced by illusions again. The mind will always generate stories; that is part of being human. The difference is that you will no longer be ruled by them. You will notice them, question them, and choose consciously whether to follow them. Over time, this skill becomes second nature. It enables you to engage with life as it truly is, rather than through layers of assumption and distortion. This is the foundation for deeper work with reality, because until you can see clearly, every attempt to create change will be built on unstable ground.

Chapter 2: The Forgotten Laws That Govern Reality

Beyond Attraction: The Three Core Laws Most People Ignore:

Most people are familiar with the concept of the Law of Attraction, even if they have never studied it in depth. The idea that like attracts like has been popularized in countless books and social media content. It promises that focusing on what you want will bring it into your life. While this principle contains truth, it is only one part of a much larger system. Relying on attraction alone often leads to disappointment because it ignores other equally powerful forces at play. These additional laws do not cancel attraction; they complete it. Without them, manifestation feels inconsistent, leaving people wondering why visualization and positive thinking sometimes work and sometimes fail.

To understand why these laws matter, consider how reality operates as an interconnected field rather than a single mechanism. Attraction describes one relationship between energy and outcome, but it does not explain why certain desires seem blocked, why effort sometimes backfires, or why opportunities appear when you least expect them. The missing pieces lie in three lesser-known principles: resonance, alignment, and inspired action. Each adds a layer of depth to the process of conscious creation, and together they form a framework that is far more reliable than attraction alone.

Resonance is the first of these overlooked laws. While attraction describes the general pull between similar energies, resonance is about the depth of that similarity. Two frequencies may appear close but fail to fully interact if they are not in harmony. This is why you can want something consciously yet still feel distant from it. On the surface, you think about the goal, but deep down, unresolved fears or conflicting beliefs create a frequency mismatch. Resonance requires coherence between conscious desire and subconscious state. Without it, manifestation efforts resemble tuning into a radio station with static — the signal is there but distorted.

The second law, alignment, extends beyond personal desire to include timing and context. Alignment is what happens when your internal readiness matches external conditions. Many people blame themselves when things do not manifest on their preferred timeline, but often the external pieces are not yet in place. Alignment recognizes that life is not only about what you want but about how your intention fits into the larger unfolding of events and relationships around you. This does not mean passively waiting. It means staying receptive and adaptable, allowing opportunities to emerge in ways you may not anticipate while remaining steady in your inner clarity.

The third law is inspired action, the bridge between inner work and tangible results. Traditional teachings often downplay this step, implying that desire alone is enough. In reality, change requires engagement. Inspired action is different from forced effort; it arises naturally when resonance and alignment are in place. It feels intuitive rather than pressured, as if life itself is guiding you toward the next step. Ignoring this law leads to stagnation. Understanding it creates momentum, allowing desires to move from possibility into form.

When you view attraction alongside resonance, alignment, and inspired action, manifestation stops being a simplistic formula and becomes a living process. Each law supports the others. Attraction sets the initial pull, resonance deepens the connection, alignment opens the right timing, and inspired action anchors the outcome into reality. Recognizing this interplay resolves the frustration many people feel when focusing on attraction alone. Resonance is often where the deepest work begins, because it reveals the subtle gaps between what you say you want and what you actually believe you can have. You might declare a desire for abundance while unconsciously holding beliefs of unworthiness or fear of judgment. These hidden currents prevent the frequency of your desire from fully harmonizing with your energy. Bringing them to light is not about shaming yourself but about creating coherence. When the inner and outer signals match, attraction stops feeling like a battle and begins to feel like gravity. The things you want are no longer being pulled in two directions; they are drawn to you naturally. Alignment introduces another layer, which is learning to trust the intelligence of timing. Many people treat delays as failures without realizing they are often evidence of rearrangement. The opportunities you seek may require preparation, not just within yourself but in the world around you. Someone you are meant to meet may not yet be ready. Circumstances may need to shift to support the outcome you want. Understanding alignment turns waiting into an active process rather than passive frustration. You remain engaged, cultivating readiness rather than forcing outcomes that are not yet viable. This shift in perspective prevents burnout and invites a steadier sense of trust in life's unfolding.

Inspired action transforms this internal clarity into movement. It is the moment where the intangible becomes tangible. Without action, even the most aligned energy remains potential rather than reality. The key is that this action does not feel forced or desperate. It arises naturally, often accompanied by a sense of calm urgency or quiet certainty. You feel pulled rather than pushed. This is what distinguishes inspired action from reactive busyness. It comes after you have tuned your internal state and are listening closely for the signals that guide you forward.

When these three laws work together, manifestation becomes less about controlling outcomes and more about partnering with the deeper intelligence woven through reality. You begin to notice how inner shifts are mirrored externally, how timing aligns without strain, and how opportunities arrive with precision you could not have planned. This is not coincidence but coherence. Life responds differently when your frequency, beliefs, and actions move in the same direction.

Recognizing these principles also dissolves much of the self-blame that accompanies failed attempts at manifestation. When attraction alone does not deliver results, people often assume they are thinking wrong or not believing hard enough. Understanding resonance, alignment, and inspired action reveals a more compassionate truth: the process is not broken; it is incomplete. With the full framework, you gain the tools to identify which element needs attention rather than abandoning the practice altogether.

Applying this understanding takes patience and self-awareness, but it pays off with stability and depth. Instead of bouncing between excitement and disappointment, you develop a steady rhythm of growth. You learn to notice when your energy is clear, when timing is ripening, and when action is needed. Over time, this becomes second nature. You stop chasing life and start engaging with it deliberately, co-creating rather than struggling against invisible currents.

This deeper perspective marks a shift from beginner-level manifestation to mastery. It bridges the gap between inspiration and grounded results, preparing you for the work ahead. In the coming chapters, these principles will continue to surface, woven through every practice and insight. As you integrate them, you will begin to experience reality not as a fixed path but as a living field that responds to your deepest alignment.

Cause, Effect, and Resonance: The Real Drivers of "Luck"

People often explain success or failure with a single word: luck. When something goes well beyond expectation, they call it good luck. When plans fall apart without warning, they call it bad luck. This explanation can feel comforting because it suggests that outcomes are random and therefore outside personal responsibility. Yet it also creates frustration, leaving people feeling powerless to influence their circumstances. If luck is random, there is nothing to study or improve. But if what we call luck is actually the visible outcome of deeper principles, it can be understood, influenced, and even cultivated.

Behind the idea of luck lie two intertwined forces: cause and effect, and resonance. Cause and effect is widely recognized but often misunderstood. In simple terms, it states that every action produces a result. Yet life is rarely as linear as we imagine. We expect immediate reactions to our efforts — work hard today, get rewarded tomorrow — and when results do not appear on that timeline, we assume nothing is happening. In reality, causes often ripple outward in complex ways, interacting with unseen factors before returning as visible outcomes.

Consider planting a seed. The moment you place it in the soil, a process begins beneath the surface. Days or weeks may pass before you see any sign of growth, but that does not mean nothing is happening. Roots are forming, systems are establishing, and conditions are aligning. Life works similarly. Actions, choices, and even subtle shifts in energy create effects that may not be visible immediately but gather momentum until they surface. Recognizing this prevents the discouragement that comes from expecting instant feedback.

Resonance adds another dimension. While cause and effect describe how actions lead to outcomes, resonance explains why similar actions can lead to very different results for different people. Two individuals may work equally hard, yet one experiences a breakthrough while the other struggles. The difference often lies in resonance — the alignment between a person's internal state and the opportunities they seek. When beliefs, emotions, and intentions harmonize with action, the effects of that action amplify. When they are fragmented, results are muted or inconsistent.

This interplay of cause, effect, and resonance is often misinterpreted as luck because it operates subtly. People see only the visible outcome — a sudden opportunity, an unexpected windfall, a chance meeting — and assume it appeared randomly. They do not see the internal work that created resonance or the chain of causes that built up over time. By understanding these principles, you begin to recognize that what seems like coincidence is often the culmination of alignment and preparation meeting opportunity.

This perspective shifts how you approach both success and setbacks. Instead of asking why some people are lucky, you begin asking what patterns create the conditions for their luck to appear. This question leads to deeper self-inquiry: Are your actions aligned with your deeper intentions? Are your beliefs supporting or contradicting what you are working toward? Are you patient enough to allow causes to mature into visible effects?

Learning to work with these dynamics requires patience, because resonance cannot be forced and cause-and-effect cycles unfold at their own pace. Yet the more aware you become of these principles, the more you notice patterns that others overlook. You begin to anticipate openings and adjust your timing. You learn to stay steady during apparent stagnation because you understand that unseen shifts often precede visible breakthroughs. This is where the perception of luck begins to dissolve and is replaced by trust in the deeper mechanics of life.

The more you examine events in your own life, the more you notice that outcomes are rarely isolated. A single success often traces back to a series of decisions, habits, and internal shifts that may have started months or even years earlier. Meeting the right person at the right time can seem accidental, but perhaps it followed from joining a community, pursuing a certain interest, or even working through fears that once kept you isolated. When you trace the thread backward, the randomness dissolves. You begin to see a pattern: preparation meeting opportunity in a way that feels seamless precisely because you were ready for it when it arrived.

Resonance magnifies this process by influencing how opportunities present themselves and how you respond to them. When your internal state is coherent — when your beliefs support your goals, and your emotional frequency reflects openness rather than scarcity — you naturally perceive possibilities that others overlook. It is not that those opportunities did not exist before; it is that your awareness was too clouded to recognize them. This explains why some people seem to be in the right place at the right time more often. Their resonance draws them toward experiences that match their internal state and primes them to act when those experiences appear.

Working with these principles requires cultivating both patience and intentionality. Patience allows you to trust that cause-and-effect cycles are unfolding even when you cannot yet see results. Intentionality ensures that the causes you set in motion are aligned with the life you want to create. Without intentionality, it is easy to send mixed signals — pursuing a goal outwardly while holding doubt inwardly. This mismatch produces scattered results and reinforces the belief that outcomes are random. Aligning thought, feeling, and action creates a unified signal that reality responds to with far greater consistency.

The skill lies in balancing action with awareness. Constantly forcing outcomes often disrupts resonance, while doing nothing prevents cause and effect from taking shape. The middle path is deliberate engagement: taking meaningful steps, observing feedback, and adjusting without attachment to rigid timelines. This allows for responsiveness rather than control. Over time, this balanced approach builds trust — not in blind luck, but in your ability to participate in the unfolding of life consciously.

One of the most liberating realizations is that setbacks are part of this process, not evidence against it. A missed opportunity may redirect you toward something more aligned. A delay may allow unseen causes to mature so that the eventual effect is stronger. This perspective reframes difficulties as feedback rather than failure. Instead of collapsing into frustration, you learn to ask what the moment is showing you about resonance and readiness. In doing so, you convert experiences that once felt discouraging into opportunities for recalibration.

As you integrate this understanding, the concept of luck begins to lose its power over you. What once felt like chance now reveals itself as interplay between preparation, perception, and timing. You realize that while you cannot control every variable in life, you can influence how prepared you are, how attuned you become, and how willing you are to act when the moment arrives. This shift creates a quiet confidence. Life may still surprise you, but those surprises feel less random and more like natural extensions of the work you have been doing within.

This awareness marks an important turning point. It transforms you from a passive observer of fortune into an active participant in the subtle mechanics that drive it. By cultivating resonance and aligning your actions with deeper intention, you begin to experience the kind of outcomes that others label lucky but that you understand as the natural result of inner and outer harmony. This is the foundation for the more advanced practices ahead, where you will learn to refine this alignment even further and work consciously with the forces that shape your reality.

How Hidden Laws Interact and Why Misalignment Creates Chaos

When people first encounter the idea of hidden laws shaping reality, they often treat them as isolated principles. They might focus exclusively on attraction, or on alignment, or on resonance, believing that mastering a single law is enough to create transformation. In practice, these laws do not operate independently. They function as parts of a single system, each influencing and amplifying the others. Ignoring this interplay is one of the main reasons people struggle with inconsistent results. They unknowingly strengthen one area while neglecting another, creating internal contradictions that manifest as chaos in their external lives.

Imagine three musicians playing different instruments without listening to one another. Each may be talented on their own, but without harmony, the result is noise. The hidden laws of reality work in much the same way. When resonance, alignment, and attraction are synchronized, life feels coherent. Opportunities appear naturally, relationships deepen, and progress accelerates with minimal resistance. When they are out of sync, the opposite occurs: confusion, stagnation, and unexpected setbacks. This misalignment is not punishment; it is feedback that something within you or your environment requires recalibration.

The first point of interaction occurs between resonance and attraction. Attraction describes the pull between similar energies, but resonance determines whether that pull is strong or weak. You might attract situations that reflect your thoughts, but without resonance — a deeper harmony between your conscious and subconscious — those situations may not stabilize. For example, someone may attract financial opportunities through visualization, but if their deeper beliefs equate wealth with danger or guilt, those opportunities either collapse or remain just out of reach. This dynamic explains why surface-level practices often feel inconsistent; they are only addressing part of the system.

Alignment adds another crucial dimension. It governs timing and context, determining whether your inner state matches the unfolding circumstances around you. Even when resonance is strong and attraction is active, misalignment can create delays or disruptions. Think of a door that opens only when multiple keys are turned at once. If inner clarity is present but external readiness is missing, the door remains closed. Recognizing this prevents unnecessary self-blame and encourages patience without passivity. Alignment is cultivated by staying attentive to life's signals and adapting rather than clinging to rigid timelines.

Misalignment can also occur when different parts of the self are at odds. The conscious mind may desire growth while the subconscious clings to safety. Emotions may oscillate between hope and fear, creating a mixed signal that reality mirrors back. This internal fragmentation is not a personal flaw but a sign of unintegrated experiences — memories, beliefs, or conditioning that have yet to be reconciled. Bringing these elements into harmony requires honesty about what you truly feel and believe, not just what you wish to feel or believe. Without this inner coherence, the laws of reality respond inconsistently, producing outcomes that feel chaotic.

Understanding the interplay of these laws reframes how you view obstacles. Instead of interpreting them as signs that manifestation does not work, you begin to see them as indicators of where alignment or resonance is missing. This shift is empowering. It transforms setbacks from sources of discouragement into opportunities for refinement. When you notice chaos, you are not being punished; you are being shown exactly where to adjust. This feedback loop, once recognized, becomes one of the most valuable tools for conscious creation.

When you start observing how these laws overlap, you begin to recognize patterns that were invisible before. Misalignment often reveals itself through repeating experiences — similar conflicts appearing in different relationships, financial patterns that cycle despite external changes, or opportunities that arise but quickly slip away. Rather than seeing these repetitions as bad luck, you can view them as signals pointing toward unresolved imbalances. This recognition alone is powerful because it shifts your focus from blaming external circumstances to exploring the internal dynamics creating them.

Bringing the laws into harmony begins with awareness. You cannot correct misalignment if you do not know it exists. Developing the habit of checking in with your internal state — noticing thoughts, emotional tone, and physical sensations — helps you detect subtle signals of discord early. For example, you might feel tension in your body when pursuing a goal that seems positive on the surface but conflicts with deeper values. That tension is not a sign to quit; it is a sign to inquire. Is this goal truly aligned, or am I chasing it out of habit, fear, or external pressure? These questions uncover the layers that surface thinking often misses.

Once awareness is established, the next step is integration. Integration means bringing different aspects of yourself into agreement so that your energy is no longer fragmented. This may involve uncovering beliefs that contradict your conscious goals, addressing unresolved fears, or updating outdated stories about what is possible. As these internal conflicts are resolved, resonance strengthens, and alignment becomes easier to maintain. The external world responds because the signal you broadcast is no longer mixed. You are no longer asking for one thing while expecting another.

Practical engagement is essential here. Hidden laws are not activated by theory alone; they respond to how you live day to day. Choices, habits, and even small acts of self-honesty accumulate into causes that eventually return as effects. When you align your actions with your internal clarity, you begin to experience coherence. This coherence is not about perfection but about consistency — showing up in a way that reinforces the reality you are choosing rather than contradicting it. Over time, this creates momentum, and what once felt chaotic begins to stabilize.

Misalignment often teaches through discomfort. Chaos is uncomfortable, but it is also informative. It reveals where you are out of sync with your deeper truth or with the unfolding of events around you. Instead of fearing chaos, you can learn to read it. Does the discomfort come from external conditions you cannot control, or from an inner conflict asking to be resolved? This kind of discernment prevents unnecessary struggle and transforms turbulence into guidance. Rather than resisting, you begin to cooperate with the feedback life is offering.

Harmony among the hidden laws does not create a life without challenges, but it does create a life with clarity. Even in difficult moments, you feel oriented rather than lost. You understand which part of the system requires attention — whether it is deepening resonance, adjusting timing, or taking inspired action. This clarity removes much of the panic that arises when results do not appear immediately. You trust the process because you understand it.

By working with these principles consciously, chaos stops being an enemy and becomes part of your evolution. It signals where refinement is needed and invites you to step into greater coherence. This is the path toward mastery: learning not just how the hidden laws work individually, but how they interact as a single, living framework. Once you embody that understanding, you move beyond the inconsistent results that frustrate so many seekers and into a more stable, empowered relationship with reality itself.

Chapter 3: Identity and the Self You Broadcast

Your Self-Concept as the Blueprint of Your Life

Everything you experience is filtered through one defining factor: the way you see yourself. This internal image — your self-concept — is not just a set of thoughts about who you are. It is the blueprint that quietly shapes how you interpret events, what you expect from life, and what you believe you deserve. Without realizing it, you are always living in harmony with this inner design, even when it contradicts what you consciously say you want.

Self-concept is formed gradually, influenced by family dynamics, cultural messages, personal experiences, and the meaning you gave to them as you grew. Early praise or criticism leaves imprints. Successes and failures become reference points for what you believe is possible. Over time, these impressions harden into identity statements: "I am capable," "I always mess things up," "I am lovable," "I am never chosen." These statements operate in the background, directing behavior and perception without conscious awareness.

What makes self-concept so powerful is that it silently dictates your expectations. If you believe deep down that you are unworthy of abundance, you may unconsciously reject opportunities that could improve your life. If you see yourself as resilient, you will naturally approach challenges differently, often finding solutions others miss. These expectations function like self-fulfilling prophecies. You are not attracting random events; you are consistently aligning with what your internal blueprint says is normal for you.

Understanding this explains why willpower alone rarely creates lasting change. People can push themselves toward a goal for a time, but if their self-concept contradicts that goal, they eventually sabotage themselves. Someone might save money diligently, only to find ways to spend it impulsively because they still see themselves as someone who "never gets ahead." Another might enter a healthy relationship but feel uncomfortable receiving love because it does not match their identity as someone who must struggle to earn approval. Change at the level of behavior is temporary unless it is supported by change at the level of identity.

This is also why affirmations and surface-level positive thinking often fail. Repeating "I am wealthy" does little if the deeper identity remains rooted in scarcity. The subconscious mind resists statements that do not align with its established blueprint. Instead of integrating, they create tension, sometimes even reinforcing the belief that the new identity is out of reach. True transformation begins not with forcing new thoughts but with uncovering and reshaping the deeper identity driving the old ones.

Reshaping self-concept requires a willingness to examine your assumptions about who you are. Much of what you believe about yourself was never consciously chosen. It was inherited, conditioned, or formed in response to events that no longer define you. By questioning these inherited stories, you create the possibility of designing a self-concept that aligns with your desired reality rather than your past. This is not about denying history; it is about reclaiming authorship of the meaning you give to it.

As you begin this work, one of the most revealing exercises is to notice how you describe yourself in everyday language. The casual statements you make — "I'm bad with money," "I don't trust people," "I always procrastinate" — are clues to the blueprint running your life. These phrases may feel harmless, but they reinforce neural pathways and energetic patterns that perpetuate the same experiences. Awareness is the first step toward rewriting them, because you cannot change what you refuse to see.

Rewriting your self-concept begins by creating space between who you believe you are and who you could be. This is not about pretending to be someone else or discarding everything that has shaped you. It is about identifying which parts of your identity genuinely serve your growth and which parts have been unconsciously inherited or adopted through pain. This distinction allows you to make deliberate choices rather than living on autopilot.

One effective way to work with this is through self-observation. Rather than trying to force change immediately, begin by watching your patterns with curiosity. Notice how you respond to compliments, challenges, or setbacks. Pay attention to the thoughts that arise when you set ambitious goals. These reactions reveal the unconscious assumptions you carry about yourself. You may find, for instance, that praise makes you uncomfortable because you secretly believe you do not deserve it, or that opportunities feel overwhelming because they contradict the identity you have grown used to.

Once these patterns surface, the next step is reconditioning. This involves gradually introducing new beliefs and behaviors that support your desired self-concept. The key word is gradual. The subconscious resists abrupt changes, but it adapts when shown consistent evidence over time. Rather than telling yourself you are entirely different overnight, demonstrate change through repeated action and reinforcement. Each time you follow through on a new habit, set a boundary, or respond in alignment with your higher vision, you build proof that the new identity is real. Over time, these repetitions become the default rather than the exception.

Another important factor is emotional congruence. Identity is not only cognitive; it is felt. If you attempt to affirm a new self-concept without addressing the emotions that contradict it, progress will stall. For example, you may want to see yourself as confident, but if old shame or fear lingers unacknowledged, that energy will subtly pull you back toward old patterns. Integrating these emotions does not mean suppressing them; it means allowing them to surface, understanding their origins, and gradually releasing the charge they hold. This emotional work stabilizes the new self-concept so it can endure beyond moments of temporary motivation.

Environment also plays a role. The people and spaces you interact with daily either reinforce your old identity or support the emerging one. If you are surrounded by reminders of past limitations, shifting your self-concept will feel like swimming against a current. This does not always require drastic changes like leaving relationships or moving cities. Often, it begins with curating smaller influences — what you read, what you consume online, the conversations you engage in — so that your environment reflects the reality you are choosing to embody.

As you refine your self-concept, life begins to mirror the shift. Circumstances that once felt out of reach become attainable because your actions, choices, and expectations are aligned. This is not magic in the sense of bypassing effort; it is the natural result of coherence. When your identity matches your desires, you stop sabotaging yourself. You recognize opportunities sooner, take action more decisively, and persist where you once would have given up.

Ultimately, transforming self-concept is not about becoming someone new but remembering who you were before fear, conditioning, and limitation took hold. It is the process of peeling away what is false and realigning with what has always been possible for you. When you live from that clarity, the blueprint guiding your life stops repeating old patterns and begins constructing something entirely different — a reality that reflects the truth of who you have chosen to become.

How Identity Shapes Relationships, Finances, and Health Automatically

Your identity is not confined to how you see yourself in isolation; it actively shapes every area of your life. The image you hold of who you are silently governs your relationships, finances, and even your physical health. This influence is so subtle that most people never realize it is happening. They believe their circumstances are the result of external forces — luck, timing, or other people's decisions — without recognizing that their self-concept has been directing the script all along.

In relationships, identity determines what you believe you deserve and how you allow others to treat you. Someone who carries an unexamined belief of unworthiness often tolerates dynamics that reinforce that belief. They may overgive in an attempt to earn love or stay silent to avoid conflict, even when silence harms them. Conversely, someone with a grounded sense of worth sets boundaries naturally. They are not immune to challenges, but they approach conflict without collapsing into self-doubt. Over time, this quiet confidence shapes the quality of their connections, drawing people who reflect the value they hold for themselves.

This dynamic explains why certain patterns repeat across different partners or friendships. The faces change, but the roles remain familiar. If you believe on some level that you must prove yourself to be loved, you will unconsciously gravitate toward relationships that require you to keep proving. Until the underlying identity shifts, the pattern continues, no matter how many surface changes you make.

The same principle applies to finances. Money does not just respond to action; it responds to the beliefs and identity behind the action. Someone who sees themselves as "bad with money" will unconsciously reinforce that story, perhaps by overspending when they receive extra income or avoiding financial planning altogether. Even ambitious people can fall into this trap if their self-concept equates wealth with selfishness or guilt. They may sabotage opportunities or settle for less than they are capable of earning, not because they lack skill, but because their internal blueprint resists expansion.

On the other hand, a person who sees themselves as capable and worthy of abundance approaches money differently. They are more likely to notice opportunities, to make long-term decisions instead of reacting impulsively, and to persist through setbacks without interpreting them as proof of failure. This is not about blind optimism; it is about identity shaping perception, and perception shaping action. The story you hold about who you are financially becomes a self-fulfilling prophecy.

Health is equally influenced by identity, though the connection is often overlooked. The way you think about your body — whether you view it as resilient or fragile, trustworthy or prone to failure — affects how you treat it and even how it responds. Someone who believes they are "always sick" may unconsciously magnify minor symptoms or neglect supportive habits because they assume decline is inevitable. In contrast, someone who identifies as healthy is more inclined to prioritize rest, nourishment, and movement, reinforcing the very state they believe they inhabit.

These influences operate automatically. You do not wake up and consciously decide to limit yourself; the blueprint simply runs in the background, filtering choices and shaping behavior. This is why people can work hard to change their habits without achieving lasting results. If the identity driving the habits remains unchanged, the old patterns eventually return. Meaningful transformation begins when you address the deeper story — the unspoken belief about who you are and what is possible for you.

Changing these deeply ingrained patterns starts with recognizing the connection between identity and behavior. Many people try to improve their relationships, finances, or health through discipline alone. They focus on surface actions — communicating better, saving more, exercising regularly — but ignore the identity driving those actions. If your self-concept contradicts the change you are trying to make, your subconscious will always pull you back toward what feels familiar. This is why people can briefly succeed with diets, budgets, or relationship resolutions only to return to old habits once motivation fades.

The most effective shift happens when identity is addressed first. When you begin to see yourself as someone who values healthy relationships, financial stability, or personal well-being, your actions naturally align with that vision. You stop forcing behaviors and start embodying them. Choosing nourishing food or setting financial goals no longer feels like a temporary effort; it feels like something that simply makes sense for who you are now.

This internal shift creates long-term consistency because you are no longer fighting against yourself.

Identity work also transforms how you interpret challenges. In relationships, a person who identifies as unworthy may view conflict as confirmation that they are failing, leading them to withdraw or overcompensate. A person who sees themselves as valuable will view the same conflict as an opportunity to clarify boundaries or deepen understanding. In finances, someone rooted in scarcity might perceive an unexpected bill as proof they can never get ahead, while someone aligned with abundance sees it as a manageable hurdle. The external event is the same; the meaning you attach to it changes everything about your response. Health follows this pattern closely. The belief that you are fragile or prone to illness can lead you to anticipate problems and interpret normal bodily sensations as warning signs, creating unnecessary stress that actually weakens resilience. Conversely, identifying as someone who is fundamentally strong encourages proactive habits like rest, movement, and self-care without fear driving them. Over time, this approach builds a sense of partnership with your body rather than conflict, supporting both physical and emotional well-being.

Redefining identity is not an overnight process. It requires consistent observation and a willingness to challenge the stories you have carried for years. The shift begins subtly, often in language. You start replacing phrases like "I am terrible with money" or "I always pick the wrong partners" with questions like "What would someone who values themselves choose here?" or "How would a financially capable version of me handle this situation?" These questions open the door to new behaviors without demanding perfection. Each small choice becomes evidence for the emerging identity, gradually making it the default.

The payoff for this work is profound. When self-concept changes, external circumstances follow. Relationships naturally become healthier because you no longer tolerate patterns that diminish you. Finances stabilize as you approach money with clarity and purpose rather than fear or avoidance. Health improves because you treat your body as something worth caring for rather than as an enemy to battle. These changes may seem subtle at first, but they compound over time, transforming not just isolated outcomes but the entire trajectory of your life.

Ultimately, identity shapes the boundaries of what you believe is possible. By redefining who you are at the deepest level, you rewrite those boundaries entirely. This does not mean you never face challenges again; it means challenges no longer define you. Instead of living in reaction to old patterns, you begin creating from a place of conscious choice, allowing every area of your life to rise to meet the truth of who you have chosen to become.

The Practical Process of Identity Shifting

Changing identity is not about forcing yourself into an entirely new persona overnight. It is about consciously evolving the internal blueprint that has quietly guided your choices and expectations for years. This process is practical, though it requires patience and consistent self-observation. The goal is not to pretend to be someone else but to align with the version of yourself that already exists beneath layers of conditioning and doubt.

The first step is awareness. You cannot shift what you cannot see. Begin by observing the way you talk to yourself about who you are. Listen to the automatic statements that arise in your mind when you face challenges or opportunities. Do you think, "I always mess this up"? Do you quietly believe, "I am not the type of person who can succeed at that"? These passing thoughts are not harmless; they reveal the current self-concept running in the background. Noticing them without judgment allows you to bring them from unconscious habit into conscious awareness, which is where change begins.

Once you identify these patterns, the next step is questioning them. Many of the beliefs you hold about yourself were formed in childhood or during emotionally charged experiences and were never revisited. Ask yourself whether these assumptions are true, or whether they simply reflect an outdated narrative you have been carrying. For example, a person who once struggled in school may still identify as "bad at learning," even if that label no longer reflects their abilities. Questioning these assumptions disrupts their power and creates space for new possibilities.

After questioning comes replacement. You do not simply eliminate an old identity; you replace it with a more aligned one. This is where intentional design begins. Decide who you are becoming and define what that version of you believes, feels, and does. The key here is specificity. Vague affirmations like "I am confident" have little impact because they do not engage the senses or emotions. Instead, imagine how confidence would feel in your body, how it would shape your posture, tone of voice, and decisions. Envisioning these details turns the new identity from an abstract idea into a lived experience.

Embodiment is the stage where identity begins to shift from concept to reality. Here, small actions become critical. Every time you behave in a way that reflects the identity you are building, you reinforce it. If you are shifting into the identity of someone who values health, choosing nourishing food or prioritizing rest is no longer a chore; it is evidence of who you are becoming. These repeated signals rewire the subconscious, gradually making the new identity feel natural rather than forced.

The process is not linear. Old patterns resurface, especially under stress. This does not mean you are failing; it means your nervous system is returning to what feels familiar. The key is to recognize these moments as opportunities to realign rather than reasons to give up. Over time, the balance tips. The new identity becomes familiar, and the old one begins to feel distant, almost like a story that belonged to someone else.

Consistency is what locks the shift into place. The subconscious learns through repetition, and identity is no exception. Each time you act in harmony with the new self-concept, you deepen the neural pathways that support it. This is why small, daily actions often create greater change than dramatic efforts followed by burnout. Incremental proof builds quiet certainty. Over time, you no longer need to remind yourself who you are becoming; you simply live as that person without thinking about it.

Another important element is emotional integration. Shifting identity can stir resistance, because the old self was built to protect you in some way. Even patterns you dislike often exist because they once felt safe. Rather than rejecting these older parts of yourself, acknowledge them. Understand what they were trying to accomplish, then reassure them that you no longer need the same strategies. This compassionate approach softens resistance and prevents the inner conflict that arises when you try to force transformation through willpower alone.

Visualization can be a valuable tool in this process, but it must be used with depth rather than as a superficial exercise. The most effective visualizations engage the senses and emotions, allowing you to experience what it feels like to live from the new identity. This goes beyond imagining outcomes; it focuses on embodying the state of being that leads to those outcomes. By repeatedly placing yourself in this emotional and mental state, you prime your nervous system to accept it as normal rather than aspirational.

The environment you inhabit also plays a significant role. Surroundings can either reinforce the old identity or support the new one. This includes the physical spaces you spend time in, the people you interact with, and the content you consume. Creating even subtle environmental cues —

reminders of who you are becoming — helps stabilize the shift. This might look like decluttering spaces that reflect outdated versions of you, curating your social media feeds to align with your values, or spending more time around people who embody the qualities you are cultivating.

Patience is essential. Identity shifts rarely happen in a single moment, even if there are breakthroughs along the way. It is easy to grow discouraged when old patterns resurface or when external results take longer to appear. Remember that what is changing is foundational; it is the framework through which you interpret and create your entire life. Giving this process the time it needs ensures the change is enduring rather than fleeting.

As the new identity takes hold, external circumstances begin to reflect the shift in ways that can feel subtle at first and profound over time. Relationships evolve because you engage from a different level of self-respect. Finances improve because you make decisions aligned with abundance rather than fear. Health stabilizes as you prioritize care rather than punishment. These changes are not separate miracles but natural consequences of embodying a different version of yourself.

Ultimately, identity shifting is not about becoming someone entirely new but about removing the layers that have obscured who you were capable of being all along. It is about reclaiming authorship over your own narrative and aligning your inner blueprint with the life you truly want to create. When that alignment is achieved, the effort of maintaining change dissolves, and what once felt like hard work becomes the natural expression of who you are.

Part II. Inner Transformation

Before you can work skillfully with the hidden laws of reality, you must address the place where those laws meet your daily life: your inner world. The principles explored in the previous section operate constantly, but how they shape your experience depends on the lens through which you perceive them. That lens is formed by your beliefs, your self-concept, and the emotional patterns you have carried for years — many of which were adopted unconsciously. Transforming these internal dynamics is the foundation for any lasting external change.

This part of the book takes you deeper into the work of alignment. Instead of focusing only on how reality responds to energy and attention, it examines how to recalibrate the inner structures that determine what kind of energy and attention you bring to life in the first place. Without this recalibration, attempts at manifestation often feel like pushing against a locked door. You may visualize or affirm new outcomes, but if your identity and subconscious beliefs remain rooted in old patterns, those efforts will clash with the signals you are broadcasting beneath the surface.

Inner transformation begins with honesty. It requires the courage to look at the assumptions you have been carrying — about who you are, what you deserve, and what is possible — and to question whether they reflect truth or conditioning. This is not an exercise in self-criticism but in self-liberation. By identifying the beliefs that keep you small, you open the door to choosing new ones that expand your capacity for growth.

Equally important is understanding that change must occur on multiple levels: cognitive, emotional, and behavioral. Knowing something intellectually is not enough; it must be felt and embodied. When your emotions align with your new understanding, and your actions consistently reflect it, identity begins to shift. This shift is not about becoming someone different but about returning to a more authentic version of yourself — one that is free from outdated narratives and more aligned with what you truly want to create.

Throughout this section, you will learn practical methods for uncovering hidden beliefs, reshaping self-concept, and cultivating emotional congruence. You will see how identity silently influences relationships, finances, health, and every decision you make. Most importantly, you will learn how to shift identity in a way that feels grounded and sustainable rather than forced. By integrating these insights, you will no longer struggle to hold onto change; change will hold onto you.

Inner transformation is where theory meets application. It is where you stop collecting ideas about hidden reality and start living them. When this internal shift occurs, external circumstances naturally begin to reflect it. What once felt like resistance turns into flow, and what once seemed distant becomes possible. This is the work that prepares you to step fully into the hidden side of reality, not as a concept, but as a lived experience.

Chapter 4: Mastering Emotional Frequency

Why Emotion, Not Thought, Determines Your Reality

For years, popular teachings about manifestation have emphasized the power of thought. The advice is often the same: think positively, visualize success, and repeat affirmations until your mind believes them. While thought certainly plays a role in shaping perception, it is not the primary driver of reality. Emotion holds far more influence. It is emotion that gives thought weight, color, and charge. Without emotion, thoughts are inert; they pass through the mind without leaving a mark. With emotion, they become signals that the subconscious and the body respond to, shaping decisions and behaviors that ripple outward into your life.

To understand why emotion is so influential, consider how the brain processes experience. Thoughts occur in the neocortex, the part of the brain responsible for logic and reasoning. Emotions, however, originate in deeper structures such as the limbic system, which evolved to prioritize survival. When emotion is strong, it overrides rational thought. This is why someone can logically know they are safe but still feel paralyzed by fear, or know they deserve love but still feel unworthy. The emotional imprint is stronger than the intellectual conclusion, and until it shifts, behavior will continue to reflect the emotional state rather than the conscious desire.

This is also why people can hold positive thoughts while still experiencing negative outcomes. They may say affirmations about abundance, but if their emotional state is rooted in anxiety about money, that anxiety will shape their behavior and perception. They will notice bills rather than opportunities, avoid financial conversations, or make choices driven by fear rather than clarity. The mind might be thinking abundance, but the body is broadcasting scarcity. Reality responds to the deeper frequency, not the surface thought.

Emotion influences reality not just internally but externally as well. Humans are wired to pick up on subtle emotional cues — tone of voice, facial expressions, body language — often more than on the actual words being spoken. These signals communicate far more than thoughts alone. When your emotional state is congruent with your intentions, you naturally exude confidence and authenticity, which influences how others respond to you. Conversely, when there is a gap between what you think and what you feel, people sense the dissonance even if they cannot articulate it. This unspoken resonance often determines the opportunities you attract or repel.

Another key factor is that emotion drives memory and learning. The experiences you remember most vividly are those tied to strong feelings — joy, pain, awe, shame. These emotional memories form the foundation of your beliefs and expectations about life. They also serve as filters for new experiences. When a situation resembles a past emotional imprint, your body reacts before your mind can process it, often reinforcing old patterns. Until those emotional imprints are addressed, they continue to shape reality automatically, regardless of how many positive thoughts you try to layer on top.

This does not mean thoughts are irrelevant. They act as gateways, often triggering emotional responses. But without shifting the emotional state itself, thought-based practices remain limited. True transformation occurs when emotion and thought work in harmony — when your feelings support your intentions rather than contradict them. This is the level where alignment begins, and where reality starts to respond in ways that feel almost effortless.

Changing emotional patterns begins with recognition rather than resistance. Most people attempt to suppress or ignore emotions they dislike, believing that avoiding fear or sadness will help them manifest better outcomes. In reality, suppressed emotions remain active beneath the surface, shaping choices in ways you cannot consciously control. The key is not to eliminate them but to acknowledge and work with them. When you bring awareness to what you feel, you create the possibility of transformation rather than repression.

A practical way to begin is by tracking emotional patterns in daily life. Notice the moments when your mood shifts suddenly — a tightening in your chest during a conversation, an unexpected wave of shame after a small mistake, a surge of relief when someone affirms you. These reactions often reveal unresolved beliefs and conditioning. Instead of judging them, view them as information. They point directly to the places where your emotional state may be out of alignment with your conscious goals.

Once recognized, emotions can be reframed and processed rather than bypassed. For example, fear often signals where growth is possible. It arises not because something is wrong but because you are stepping beyond what feels familiar. Interpreting fear this way turns it from an obstacle into a guide. Similarly, emotions like anger or envy can highlight unmet needs or unclaimed desires. By exploring what these feelings are trying to communicate, you turn them into tools for clarity rather than barriers to progress.

The body plays a critical role in this process. Emotions are not just mental events; they are physiological experiences stored in the nervous system. This is why techniques that involve the body — breathwork, grounding exercises, mindful movement — can be so effective in shifting emotional states. By calming the body, you calm the emotional charge that fuels reactive patterns. Over time, this practice creates space between stimulus and response, allowing you to choose differently rather than repeat old habits.

As emotional regulation improves, alignment becomes easier to maintain. Positive emotions like gratitude, joy, and calm are not just pleasant; they are powerful signals that harmonize your internal state with the outcomes you desire. When you cultivate these emotions consistently, you create a baseline frequency that naturally attracts experiences aligned with it. This does not mean forcing happiness or ignoring pain. It means gradually training your system to return to balance, even when life is unpredictable.

Integrating emotional work into manifestation also prevents the frustration many people feel when results are slow. If you have been thinking positive thoughts but still feeling stuck, it is likely because the emotional state has not shifted. Addressing emotion closes that gap. It aligns your inner and outer worlds, allowing thought-based practices like visualization and intention-setting to actually take root. When feelings support beliefs, you stop sending mixed signals to reality, and your efforts gain momentum.

Ultimately, mastering emotion is not about achieving constant bliss but about developing emotional coherence. This coherence allows you to remain grounded and intentional regardless of external circumstances. It is what transforms manifestation from an intellectual exercise into a lived experience. When your emotions and thoughts finally point in the same direction, life responds in kind, and change that once felt elusive begins to unfold naturally.

The Frequency Ladder: Moving From Fear to Flow

Emotions can feel chaotic when experienced without structure. One moment you feel anxious and closed off, the next inspired and optimistic, only to fall back into frustration when circumstances shift. This fluctuation is natural, but it becomes problematic when you have no framework to understand where you are and how to shift. The concept of a frequency ladder offers that framework. It allows you to identify your emotional state, understand its impact on your perception, and deliberately climb toward states that foster clarity, creativity, and alignment.

At the base of this ladder are the emotions associated with fear and contraction. These include shame, guilt, resentment, and hopelessness. When you are in this range, your focus narrows. You interpret events through the lens of survival, scanning for danger rather than possibility. This state is not wrong — it evolved to keep you safe — but it is limited. In fear, your nervous system prioritizes short-term protection over long-term growth, making it difficult to imagine new opportunities or trust your intuition.

Above fear lies anger and frustration, which, while uncomfortable, actually carry more energy. Anger signals that a boundary has been crossed or that something is misaligned. It propels action in a way that fear cannot. Many people misinterpret anger as negative, but it often marks the beginning of upward movement on the ladder. Where fear is frozen, anger wants change. Learning to channel this energy constructively — rather than suppressing it or letting it explode — is a pivotal step toward higher frequencies.

As you move further upward, you encounter neutrality and acceptance. This is the middle range of the ladder, where emotional charge softens. In neutrality, you stop fighting what is and begin observing without judgment. From this vantage point, possibilities that were invisible in fear or anger start to emerge. You are not yet euphoric or overflowing with gratitude, but you are steady enough to make intentional choices. Neutrality is underrated precisely because it lacks intensity, yet it is often the bridge that makes higher states accessible.

Beyond neutrality lies willingness, optimism, and trust. In this range, the nervous system relaxes enough to perceive opportunities clearly and engage with them without constant doubt. You begin to feel a sense of cooperation with life rather than opposition to it. These emotions are expansive; they invite creativity and foster resilience. Setbacks are still present, but they no longer define you. You start to recognize them as temporary rather than permanent, and that recognition changes how you respond.

At the highest levels of the ladder are states often described as flow: joy, peace, love, and deep gratitude. Here, your inner and outer worlds feel synchronized. You are not forcing outcomes but participating in them fluidly. Time can seem to slow or speed up, and decisions feel effortless. This is not a static destination but a dynamic state that arises when the lower rungs of the ladder have been acknowledged and integrated rather than bypassed.

Understanding the frequency ladder is valuable because it removes the pressure to leap from fear to joy instantly. It shows that emotional transformation is progressive. You do not need to force yourself into bliss when you are in despair; you only need to find the next rung up.

The process of climbing the ladder begins with awareness rather than judgment. Recognizing where you are emotionally is not an admission of failure; it is a starting point. Many people resist acknowledging fear, shame, or anger because they believe doing so will trap them there. In reality, suppression prolongs those states, while honest awareness creates the possibility of movement. Simply naming what you feel begins to loosen its grip.

Once you have identified your current state, the next step is finding the smallest possible shift upward. If you are in fear, the goal is not immediate joy but perhaps frustration or determination — emotions that carry more energy and begin to mobilize you. If you are in anger, moving toward neutrality or curiosity is often realistic. This incremental approach prevents overwhelm. It also aligns with how the nervous system works; small shifts are sustainable, while forced leaps trigger resistance.

A useful way to support this progression is by focusing on practices that match the rung you are on rather than the rung you wish you were on. In lower emotional states, grounding techniques such as deep breathing or sensory awareness calm the body enough to create safety. In middle states, reflection and reframing become powerful — journaling, perspective shifts, and self-inquiry help integrate lessons and release tension. At higher rungs, creative expression, gratitude practices, and visualization can amplify alignment without feeling hollow or forced. Matching the practice to the emotional state prevents dissonance and builds trust with yourself.

The frequency ladder also reveals why bypassing emotions rarely works. Attempting to jump straight to love or gratitude without addressing underlying fear or resentment creates internal conflict. Part of you feels pressured to perform positivity while another part remains unresolved. This split results in fragile progress that collapses under stress. Acknowledging and integrating each rung creates resilience. The shift to flow is genuine because it includes rather than excludes your full emotional spectrum.

Another important aspect of this process is understanding that movement is rarely linear. You may climb several rungs and then temporarily slide back during stress or transition. This is not regression but an invitation to strengthen your capacity to realign. Each time you return to higher states more quickly, you reinforce the pathways that make flow more accessible in the future. Over time, what once felt like extraordinary emotional balance becomes your baseline.

As you stabilize in higher frequencies, your relationship to life changes fundamentally. Problems do not vanish, but your perception of them transforms. Instead of seeing challenges as evidence of failure, you begin to view them as opportunities for refinement and growth. Fear still arises occasionally, but it no longer dictates your choices. You learn to navigate discomfort without collapsing into it, which creates a quiet confidence that radiates into every area of your life.

Living in flow is not about maintaining constant euphoria. It is about staying connected to a deeper sense of trust, even in uncertainty. The frequency ladder is the map that helps you return to that trust again and again. By learning to identify your emotional state and deliberately move upward, you build a practical path to alignment — one that makes fear a doorway rather than a prison and transforms daily life into an unfolding dialogue with reality itself.

Practical Tools to Regulate and Elevate Emotional States

Shifting emotional states is not only about understanding why feelings arise but also knowing how to regulate and elevate them in real time. Insight without application can leave you stuck in cycles of awareness without progress. When you learn to work directly with your emotions, you begin to influence your internal state at will, rather than waiting for external circumstances to improve. This skill is foundational to living in alignment because it turns emotional regulation into a deliberate choice rather than a reaction.

The first step in regulation is grounding. When emotions escalate — whether fear, anger, or anxiety — the nervous system shifts into survival mode. In this state, reasoning becomes secondary, and impulses dominate. Grounding techniques interrupt this automatic response by anchoring your awareness in the present. One of the simplest methods is conscious breathing: inhaling deeply into the lower belly, holding briefly, and exhaling slowly. This pattern signals safety to the body, gradually lowering stress hormones and restoring clarity. Even a few cycles can create enough space to respond rather than react.

Sensory grounding is another effective method. Engaging the senses pulls attention out of spiraling thoughts and into the tangible present. Noticing the texture of an object in your hand, focusing on ambient sounds, or feeling your feet press against the ground are small actions that communicate stability to the nervous system. While these may seem simple, their cumulative effect is significant, especially when practiced consistently during moments of emotional intensity.

Beyond immediate regulation, elevation requires cultivating emotional states that support higher alignment. One of the most powerful ways to do this is through gratitude, but not in the superficial sense of listing things you "should" be grateful for. Effective gratitude practice engages emotion, not obligation. Instead of reciting generic phrases, choose one or two specific experiences and immerse yourself in them fully. Recall sensory details, the emotions they evoked, and the meaning they carried. This depth transforms gratitude from intellectual acknowledgment into embodied resonance, raising your emotional frequency in a lasting way.

Movement also plays a critical role in elevating emotion. Emotions are not purely mental; they are stored and expressed through the body. Physical practices such as walking, stretching, or mindful exercise release stagnant energy and stimulate neurochemicals that naturally improve mood. This is why movement can often shift emotional states faster than purely cognitive strategies. Even a brief change in posture — standing taller, opening the chest, loosening the jaw — signals a shift to the brain, influencing how you feel and perceive.

Visualization bridges both regulation and elevation. When practiced with presence, it can calm heightened emotions and inspire higher ones. Effective visualization is multisensory: you do not simply imagine an outcome; you imagine being in it. What do you hear, smell, touch, and feel emotionally in that scenario? The nervous system responds to vivid imagery as if it were real, which is why athletes and performers use visualization to prepare for peak performance. Applied to emotional alignment, it conditions the body and mind to experience higher frequencies before they manifest externally.

Over time, these practices create a foundation of emotional stability that allows you to navigate challenges without being pulled off center. This stability does not mean you stop feeling intense emotions; it means you stop being controlled by them. Even when fear or anger arises, you have tools to meet those states, work with them, and move through them rather than staying stuck. The nervous system learns that discomfort is not a threat, which dramatically expands your capacity to handle uncertainty.

Journaling can deepen this work by providing clarity about what is happening beneath the surface. Writing out raw thoughts and emotions externalizes them, making it easier to see patterns that might otherwise remain unconscious. This is especially helpful when navigating recurring emotional loops — fears about money, feelings of inadequacy in relationships, or persistent frustration about progress. By observing these patterns on paper, you can identify the beliefs fueling them and begin to reframe or release them rather than unconsciously reinforcing them.

Another powerful yet often overlooked tool is deliberate micro-pausing throughout the day. Emotional regulation is most effective when it becomes proactive rather than reactive. Taking brief pauses to check in with yourself — noticing your breath, posture, and current feeling state — helps prevent emotional buildup before it becomes overwhelming. These micro-pauses also create moments of choice: an opportunity to redirect attention toward what supports alignment rather than what reinforces stress.

As you grow more skilled in regulating emotions, the focus naturally shifts to sustaining elevated states. This involves cultivating habits that nourish the nervous system consistently rather than relying solely on tools during crises. Restorative sleep, balanced nutrition, and mindful exposure to uplifting environments all contribute to emotional resilience. These foundational practices might seem mundane, but they create the physiological conditions for emotional coherence, making higher frequencies easier to access and maintain.

Community and connection amplify this process. Emotions are contagious; being around people who embody calm, gratitude, or inspiration helps entrain your own state toward similar frequencies. This is not about seeking perfection in others but about surrounding yourself with relationships that support growth rather than pull you back into old patterns. The nervous system co-regulates with those around it, which is why intentional community can accelerate emotional transformation.

Perhaps the most important element is patience. Elevating emotional states is not about forcing constant positivity but about learning to navigate the full range of human experience without losing your center. Progress is measured less by how often you feel blissful and more by how quickly you can return to balance after being thrown off course. Each time you regulate effectively, you strengthen the pathways that make alignment more accessible in the future.

These tools, when practiced consistently, transform emotional regulation from a reactive coping mechanism into an active way of living. Rather than waiting for ideal circumstances to feel stable or inspired, you create those conditions internally. This shift empowers you to engage with reality from a place of choice rather than compulsion, allowing external events to mirror the inner balance you have cultivated. Over time, this becomes the default state — not because life has become perfect, but because you have learned to meet it from a place of grounded clarity and intentional flow.

Chapter 5: The Subconscious Operating System

How Early Programming Shapes 95% of Your Reality

Most of what you believe to be conscious choice is actually shaped by patterns formed long before you were aware of them. Research in neuroscience and developmental psychology shows that the subconscious mind governs the majority of your daily thoughts, emotions, and behaviors. This subconscious framework is largely built in childhood, when your brain is most impressionable and your sense of self is still forming. By the time you reach adulthood, these early programs operate automatically, quietly influencing how you interpret life, what you expect from others, and even what you believe is possible for you.

During the first seven years of life, the brain operates primarily in slower wave states, similar to hypnosis. This heightened suggestibility is nature's way of helping children learn rapidly from their environment. It allows them to absorb language, social norms, and survival skills without constant instruction. But this openness also means they internalize beliefs indiscriminately. A parent's passing comment, a teacher's reaction, or a single emotionally charged experience can become embedded as truth, even if it was inaccurate or unintentional.

These early impressions form the blueprint for your self-concept and worldview. If you grew up hearing that money was scarce, you may unconsciously equate financial success with danger or greed. If love was conditional on achievement, you may believe you must constantly prove your worth to be accepted. These beliefs rarely appear as conscious thoughts; they live beneath awareness, shaping behavior through subtle biases and automatic responses.

The influence of early programming is not limited to personal narratives. Cultural and societal messages also imprint deeply during childhood. Media, education, and community values all communicate unspoken rules about what is acceptable or possible. A child raised in an environment that views ambition as selfish will approach opportunity differently than one raised to see ambition as admirable. These collective imprints combine with personal experiences to form a complex map of reality that feels natural, even when it is restrictive.

Understanding this process explains why change often feels difficult. You may consciously want something different — a healthier relationship, financial freedom, inner peace — yet find yourself sabotaging progress or returning to old patterns. This is not a failure of willpower; it is the subconscious attempting to maintain familiarity. The brain equates what is familiar with what is safe, even if that familiarity is painful. Until the underlying programming is examined and reconditioned, new habits and goals struggle to take root.

Becoming aware of early programming does not mean blaming parents or revisiting every childhood memory. It is about recognizing that much of what drives you was inherited, not chosen. This recognition is liberating. It means the limitations you experience are not personal flaws but learned patterns — and what is learned can be unlearned. Awareness opens the door to rewriting the blueprint, replacing outdated survival strategies with beliefs that support growth and alignment.

Reprogramming begins with observation rather than force. Attempting to override old patterns through willpower alone rarely works, because willpower operates in the conscious mind while the subconscious runs on automatic. The first step is noticing where patterns appear: recurring conflicts in relationships, familiar struggles with money, or persistent feelings of inadequacy that seem disconnected from present circumstances. These patterns are clues pointing toward the beliefs installed early in life.

Journaling can be especially powerful in uncovering these hidden layers. Writing about triggering situations and then asking why they affect you so deeply often leads to memories or associations from childhood. For example, anxiety about being criticized at work may trace back to experiences of harsh judgment in school or at home. Recognizing this connection softens the present response because you understand it is not entirely about what is happening now — it is also about what was learned then.

Once you identify the belief, questioning it is essential. Most early programming was never consciously chosen and often does not hold up to adult scrutiny. A child may interpret a parent's absence as "I am unlovable," when in reality the absence was due to external circumstances. Bringing adult perspective to these beliefs reveals their inaccuracy and creates space for new interpretations. This is not about rewriting history but about reclaiming the authority to decide what those experiences mean today.

Replacing old programming requires repetition and emotional engagement. The subconscious learns through felt experience rather than logic alone. Visualizing yourself responding differently in familiar situations, practicing self-compassion in moments of stress, and reinforcing new beliefs through consistent action all signal to the subconscious that the old pattern is no longer relevant. Over time, the brain forms new neural pathways, making the updated response feel natural rather than forced.

Environment plays a critical role in supporting this shift. Surrounding yourself with people, information, and experiences that reflect your new identity accelerates reprogramming by providing constant reinforcement. Conversely, staying immersed in environments that mirror your old patterns makes change more difficult, as the subconscious continues to receive mixed signals. This is why transformation often involves reevaluating relationships, habits, and daily inputs to ensure they align with who you are becoming.

Patience is vital in this process. Because early programming is so deeply ingrained, it rarely changes overnight. Progress often unfolds in layers — first noticing the pattern, then interrupting it, and eventually replacing it. Each step matters, even when results are subtle. With time, you will find yourself responding to situations differently without having to think about it. That shift is the clearest sign that reprogramming has taken hold.

Ultimately, understanding the impact of early programming is not about dwelling on the past but about reclaiming the present. When you see that much of what you considered "just the way I am" was actually learned, you gain permission to choose differently. The moment you begin replacing inherited limits with intentional beliefs, you stop living on autopilot and start shaping reality from a place of conscious choice.

Spotting Hidden Scripts That Sabotage Your Desires

Much of what holds people back from creating the life they want is not conscious resistance but unconscious programming. These hidden scripts are deeply ingrained patterns of belief and behavior that operate automatically. They were formed by past experiences and often feel so familiar that they go unnoticed. Yet they quietly determine what opportunities you notice, what risks you avoid, and what you believe is possible for you. Until these scripts are identified, they continue to play out in the background, shaping reality without your awareness.

Hidden scripts are not inherently malicious. They were often created as survival strategies. A child who learns that staying quiet avoids conflict may grow into an adult who suppresses their needs in relationships. Someone who grew up in financial instability may unconsciously equate wealth with danger or shame, keeping them from pursuing opportunities that could improve their life. These responses made sense at the time they were formed, but when left unexamined, they continue to run long after they have served their purpose.

The challenge with hidden scripts is that they masquerade as truth. Because they have been repeated so many times, they feel like objective reality rather than inherited belief. You might think, "I'm just not lucky," or "People always leave," without realizing those statements are interpretations rather than facts. The subconscious mind prefers consistency, so it will filter information to confirm what it already believes. This confirmation bias makes it difficult to notice when a script is active, because your experiences appear to validate it.

Spotting these patterns begins with observation. Pay attention to recurring themes in your life — the kinds of relationships you attract, the financial ceilings you hit, the emotions that resurface in moments of stress. If you find yourself facing similar challenges despite different circumstances, that repetition is a clue. It suggests an underlying script is influencing your choices and reactions.

Another way to uncover hidden scripts is by examining your emotional triggers. Strong emotional reactions, especially those that seem disproportionate to the situation, often point to deeper programming. For example, an intense fear of failure might trace back to early experiences of being shamed for mistakes. A deep discomfort with praise might reveal a belief that visibility is unsafe. By following the emotion to its root, you begin to see the story driving it.

Language offers additional insight. The phrases you use in self-talk or conversation — "I always mess this up," "People like me can't do that," "Nothing ever works out" — reveal assumptions operating below awareness. These statements may sound casual, but they expose the underlying narrative about what you expect from life. Becoming conscious of this language is the first step in challenging it.

Recognizing a script does not immediately erase it, but it shifts your relationship to it. The moment you see the pattern, you create space between stimulus and response. You realize you have been operating on autopilot rather than making deliberate choices. That awareness alone is powerful. It transforms the script from an invisible director of your life into something you can observe, question, and eventually rewrite.

Once you have identified a script, the next step is to observe how it shows up in real time. Patterns are often clearest in the moments when you feel resistance. You might notice yourself pulling back just as an opportunity arises, procrastinating on a task that would move you forward, or discounting praise that challenges your self-image. These moments reveal the script trying to maintain the familiar, even if that familiar state is limiting. The act of noticing interrupts the cycle, making it possible to choose differently.

Curiosity is a powerful ally in this process. Rather than judging the script or labeling it as wrong, approach it with the question, "Where did this come from?" and "What is it trying to protect me from?" Many hidden scripts began as ways to avoid pain or gain approval. By understanding their origin, you reduce their hold over you. The goal is not to fight these parts of yourself but to update them, acknowledging that the strategies that once helped you survive are no longer necessary for the life you are creating now.

Practical reflection exercises can make this work tangible. One approach is to map the script's influence across different areas of your life. For example, if you identify a belief that "I have to do everything on my own," consider how it impacts your career, relationships, and personal well-being. Does it prevent you from delegating at work? Does it make intimacy feel unsafe? Does it lead to burnout because you avoid asking for help? Seeing the ripple effect helps you recognize how pervasive the pattern is and why shifting it will create such profound change.

As you explore these patterns, it is common to encounter resistance or even grief. Realizing how long you have lived under a limiting belief can stir regret or anger toward yourself or others. These emotions are part of the process. Allowing them to surface without judgment is essential to releasing them. Transformation does not come from bypassing discomfort but from meeting it with honesty and compassion. In this space, healing becomes possible because you are no longer fighting your own experience.

Bringing new awareness to hidden scripts also changes how you interpret setbacks. Instead of seeing challenges as evidence that you are failing, you can view them as opportunities to practice responding differently. A recurring situation that once triggered hopelessness becomes a chance to choose curiosity. A financial obstacle that once activated scarcity thinking becomes an invitation to strengthen trust in your ability to adapt. Each repetition becomes less about the outcome and more about reinforcing the new narrative you are consciously building.

Over time, this awareness creates freedom. What once felt like fate begins to feel like choice. The familiar cycles lose their power because you are no longer unconsciously participating in them. Instead, you respond with intentionality, aligning your decisions with the future you are creating rather than the past you are repeating. This is the turning point where internal shifts begin to manifest externally. Relationships improve, opportunities expand, and life begins to mirror the new scripts you have chosen.

Spotting these hidden narratives is not a one-time event but an ongoing practice. As you grow, new layers reveal themselves. Each one offers a deeper invitation to align your inner world with the reality you desire to create. By continuing this work, you move from being shaped by unconscious programming to becoming the conscious author of your life — and in that shift, your ability to manifest what you truly want becomes exponentially greater.

Rewriting the Subconscious With Proven Techniques

Shifting subconscious programming is not about forcing yourself to think differently for a few days. It is about creating new neural and emotional patterns strong enough to override the ones that have been operating for years. This process takes more than intellectual understanding. The subconscious learns through repetition, emotion, and embodied experience. To rewrite it, you need practices that speak the language of the subconscious rather than relying only on logic or willpower.

The first step is creating a clear target. Without a defined vision of the identity or belief you want to install, the subconscious has nothing to anchor to. This clarity is not just about outcomes, like earning more money or attracting a partner, but about the inner state that naturally produces those outcomes. Ask yourself who you would be if you already lived the reality you want. How would you think, feel, and act? These qualities become the blueprint you are working to integrate.

Once this vision is defined, repetition becomes essential. The subconscious accepts ideas as true through frequency and familiarity. Every belief you currently hold was reinforced over time until it became automatic. Rewriting them follows the same principle: consistent exposure to the new pattern until it feels normal. This can be done through affirmations, visualization, and behavioral rehearsal, but the key is engaging emotionally rather than mechanically. Repeating words without feeling rarely creates change.

Visualization is particularly powerful because the brain responds to vivid imagery almost as if it were real. When you imagine yourself acting from the new identity — confident in a meeting, calm under stress, open in a relationship — your nervous system begins wiring those pathways as if you have already lived them. The more sensory detail you include, the stronger the imprint. Feel the emotion of success, hear the sounds, notice the physical sensations in your body. This level of immersion communicates to the subconscious that this reality is safe and familiar.

Another proven method is anchoring new beliefs to physical action. The subconscious associates experiences with movement and sensation. Combining a new thought with a deliberate gesture, posture, or breath pattern strengthens its impact. For example, standing tall and breathing deeply while affirming self-trust signals both mind and body to integrate the belief. Over time, repeating this pairing creates a conditioned response, making it easier to access the new state during challenges.

Working with the subconscious also requires addressing resistance. Old patterns do not disappear overnight; they often surface as doubt, discomfort, or self-sabotage. Recognizing this as part of the process rather than a sign of failure prevents you from abandoning the work prematurely. When resistance arises, instead of forcing it away, acknowledge it and reaffirm the direction you are choosing. This practice builds trust with yourself and teaches the subconscious that growth is safe, even when unfamiliar.

The most profound changes occur when mental rehearsal is paired with real-world application. Acting in alignment with the identity you are cultivating sends the strongest signal to the subconscious because it experiences evidence rather than theory. Each time you behave in a way that contradicts an old belief and supports the new one, you reinforce the emerging pattern. Small consistent actions are more effective than grand gestures. A single conversation where you express your needs, a single day of following through on a commitment, or a single moment of choosing calm over reactivity provides tangible proof of the new reality you are building.

Emotional intensity also accelerates reprogramming. The subconscious records experiences more deeply when they are linked to strong feelings. This is why emotionally charged events, both positive and negative, are remembered so vividly. You can harness this principle by deliberately infusing positive emotional charge into new patterns. Celebrate small wins rather than dismissing them. Feel the satisfaction of progress rather than rushing to the next goal. When gratitude or pride is layered onto new actions, the subconscious encodes them more quickly as part of your identity.

Timing plays a role as well. The subconscious is most receptive in transitional states — moments when brainwave activity slows, such as right before sleep or immediately upon waking. Using these windows for visualization or affirmations can amplify their impact because the critical, analytical part of the mind is quieter. This is why practices like evening journaling or morning intention setting are especially effective; they meet the subconscious when it is most open to suggestion.

Addressing old patterns often requires releasing the emotional charge they carry. Techniques like somatic awareness, breathwork, or guided memory reprocessing allow you to revisit past experiences without becoming trapped in them. By observing the old memory from a grounded state, you teach your nervous system that the event is over and no longer defines you. This release creates space for new associations to take root, making room for updated beliefs about who you are and what is possible.

Environment remains a crucial factor in sustaining subconscious shifts. If your surroundings constantly reinforce the old narrative, transformation requires more effort. Curating what you expose yourself to — from the conversations you engage in to the media you consume — ensures that your external world supports the internal changes you are making. Surrounding yourself with people who reflect and encourage your growth accelerates integration, as the subconscious naturally adapts to the norms of the group you identify with.

Patience is perhaps the most underrated component of this work. Subconscious patterns have been running for years, often decades. Expecting them to dissolve in days creates unnecessary frustration and self-criticism. Progress often appears gradually, revealed in subtle shifts — a calmer response to a familiar trigger, a willingness to try something new, a quiet sense of trust replacing constant doubt. These changes may seem small in the moment but compound into profound transformation over time.

The reward of this process is freedom. As you rewrite the subconscious, you are no longer bound by outdated survival strategies. Your choices become intentional rather than reactive. Life begins to reflect who you truly are, not who you were taught to be. This is the foundation of lasting manifestation: a mind and body aligned with the reality you are consciously creating.

Chapter 6: Removing Resistance and Hidden Blocks

Understanding Resistance: The Invisible Force Against Change

Every time you attempt to change something significant in your life, an invisible force seems to rise up to stop you. It shows up as procrastination, self-doubt, distraction, or even physical exhaustion. Sometimes it looks like external obstacles appearing at the worst possible moment. This force is resistance. It is not random or malicious. It is the natural reaction of your subconscious mind to anything unfamiliar.

The subconscious is designed to keep you safe, and it equates safety with what is known. Even if your current circumstances are uncomfortable, they are predictable, and the brain values predictability. When you introduce change — a new belief, habit, or identity — the subconscious registers it as a potential threat. It triggers discomfort to pull you back toward what feels familiar. This is why resistance often intensifies right when you are closest to a breakthrough. The mind is trying to protect you from what it perceives as risk, even if the change is positive.

Resistance manifests in subtle and obvious ways. Sometimes it is loud, like an inner voice shouting reasons you will fail. Other times it is quiet, showing up as sudden fatigue, forgetfulness, or distraction whenever you try to work on your goal. It can even disguise itself as logic, convincing you to wait for the "right time" or gather more information before acting. The sophistication of resistance lies in its ability to blend in with rational thinking, making it hard to identify as a protective mechanism rather than objective truth.

Understanding resistance begins with noticing its patterns. Pay attention to when it appears. Does it show up every time you start a new project, set a boundary, or take a risk? Does it flare up right after moments of progress? Recognizing these patterns helps you see that resistance is not a personal flaw or a sign that something is wrong. It is simply the subconscious attempting to maintain equilibrium.

This awareness changes the way you relate to resistance. Instead of treating it as an enemy to fight, you can view it as feedback. It signals that you are leaving your comfort zone and approaching growth. The intensity of resistance often mirrors the significance of the change you are attempting. A small adjustment might create mild discomfort, while a deep identity shift can trigger fear, doubt, or even physical tension. Knowing this allows you to meet resistance with curiosity rather than panic.

The key is not eliminating resistance but learning to navigate it. Many people abandon their goals because they assume resistance means they are on the wrong path. In reality, it often means they are on exactly the right one. The presence of resistance does not predict failure; it marks the threshold of transformation. By expecting it and preparing for it, you remove its power to derail you.

One of the most effective ways to work with resistance is to remove the judgment around it. When you view it as proof of weakness, you create additional layers of shame that amplify the very discomfort you are trying to overcome. Acknowledging resistance as a protective reflex allows you to approach it with understanding. It is not evidence that you are broken; it is evidence that you are stepping into unfamiliar territory. This shift in perspective makes it easier to stay committed even when the process feels uncomfortable.

Bringing awareness to the body can also help diffuse resistance. Physical sensations often accompany mental pushback — tightness in the chest, shallow breathing, tension in the shoulders. By noticing these sensations without trying to fix them immediately, you create a pause between stimulus and reaction. Simple grounding techniques, like deep breathing or feeling your feet on the floor, send signals of safety to the nervous system. Over time, this calms the subconscious response and reduces the intensity of resistance during future attempts at change.

Breaking change into smaller steps is another powerful strategy. The subconscious resists dramatic shifts but adapts more easily to incremental ones. Instead of overhauling every aspect of your life at once, focus on manageable actions that build confidence and familiarity. Each successful step weakens the hold of old patterns and reinforces the new identity you are creating. This approach transforms resistance from an overwhelming barrier into a series of challenges you can navigate one at a time.

It is also valuable to examine the story resistance is telling you. Often, the mind creates narratives to justify staying in the familiar: "I'm not ready," "It's too late," or "I'll start when I have more time." Questioning these assumptions exposes their flaws. Are they based on facts, or are they protective stories designed to keep you safe? The moment you recognize them as stories rather than truths, you gain the freedom to act in spite of them.

Community can play a significant role in overcoming resistance. When you surround yourself with people who normalize growth and support your goals, the subconscious begins to view change as safe rather than threatening. Encouragement and accountability help you stay anchored when your own doubts are loudest. Conversely, being around those who reinforce old patterns can intensify resistance, making it harder to sustain momentum. Intentionally choosing supportive environments accelerates progress and reduces the isolation that resistance often thrives on.

Finally, patience is essential. Resistance does not disappear in a single breakthrough; it tends to resurface at each new level of growth. Recognizing this as part of the process prevents discouragement. Over time, you will notice that the intensity of resistance decreases. The more you confront it and move through it, the less control it has over your decisions. What once felt paralyzing becomes a familiar signal that you are on the edge of expansion.

By learning to recognize, interpret, and navigate resistance, you turn what once felt like an obstacle into an ally. Instead of being derailed by discomfort, you come to expect it and even welcome it as confirmation that you are moving toward something meaningful. This understanding transforms the process of change from a battle into a partnership, allowing you to cross thresholds that once seemed impossible and step fully into the life you have been working to create.

Detecting Subtle Signs of Self-Sabotage

Self-sabotage is often imagined as dramatic and obvious — abandoning a project right before it succeeds or blowing up a relationship out of fear. In reality, the most damaging forms of self-sabotage are subtle. They operate quietly, woven into daily habits and thought patterns so familiar that you do not recognize them as obstacles. This subtlety is what makes them dangerous. Because they masquerade as normal behavior or even self-protection, they continue unchecked, undermining progress while you wonder why you feel stuck.

At its core, self-sabotage arises when your conscious goals conflict with subconscious beliefs. You might want financial abundance, yet carry an inherited belief that wealth creates isolation. You may crave a healthy relationship but still identify as unworthy of love. When actions are taken toward the conscious goal, the subconscious steps in to restore what feels familiar. This creates behaviors that seem irrational on the surface — procrastination, avoidance, or even sudden loss of motivation — but make perfect sense when viewed through the lens of self-preservation.

Subtle sabotage often appears in the form of delay. You tell yourself you will start tomorrow, or once conditions are perfect. This pattern can feel harmless because it is disguised as preparation. In truth, endless preparation prevents momentum. Waiting for perfect timing or flawless readiness is the subconscious' way of avoiding risk. The delay feels justified, yet it keeps you in the safety of inaction, reinforcing the very beliefs you are trying to outgrow.

Another subtle form is minimizing success. When small wins happen, you downplay them or dismiss them as luck. This robs your subconscious of the reinforcement it needs to adopt a new identity. Celebrating incremental progress is crucial for rewiring belief systems, yet many people skip this step, unknowingly perpetuating the old narrative that they are incapable of change.

Self-sabotage also hides in overcommitment. Saying yes to everything dilutes focus and ensures nothing receives your full attention. This pattern may be framed as ambition or generosity, but it often stems from discomfort with stillness or fear of confronting deeper goals. Constant busyness creates the illusion of productivity while preventing meaningful progress.

A more insidious version is seeking external chaos just as internal order begins to form. This might look like starting unnecessary conflicts, overindulging in distractions, or taking impulsive actions that create problems to solve. The subconscious equates calm with unfamiliarity and unconsciously stirs turbulence to return to a state it recognizes. This can happen in relationships, finances, or personal routines — the moment things start going well, something "accidentally" disrupts them.

Even thoughts can become a form of sabotage. Persistent self-criticism, catastrophizing about the future, or replaying worst-case scenarios all prime the nervous system to stay in survival mode. These mental habits rarely feel extreme; they present as caution or realism. Yet they erode confidence, making aligned action feel riskier than it is. Over time, this quiet mental background noise shapes decisions and subtly keeps you aligned with old limitations rather than new possibilities.

Recognizing these patterns is only possible when you slow down enough to observe them without defensiveness. Most people rush through their days on autopilot, assuming their choices are deliberate when they are actually habitual. Creating moments of reflection allows you to notice the disconnect between your intentions and your actions. Journaling at the end of the day, for example, can reveal small ways you deviated from your stated goals — skipping an important call, indulging in procrastination disguised as research, or retreating from opportunities that felt overwhelming. These minor decisions, repeated over time, are what maintain old identities.

Paying attention to emotional cues can also uncover sabotage. Feelings of sudden fatigue, irritation, or vague discomfort when approaching growth are not random. They are signals of internal conflict. Your body is telling you that the new path is colliding with an old belief. Instead of interpreting this as a reason to stop, you can treat it as a signpost pointing directly to the subconscious programming that needs attention. Every moment of resistance carries information about what part of you fears change.

One of the most overlooked signs of sabotage is rationalizing mediocrity. It often shows up as subtle self-talk: "This is good enough," or "Maybe I don't really need that." While contentment can be healthy, this form of settling usually emerges right before a breakthrough. The subconscious tries to convince you that pursuing more is unnecessary because staying where you are feels safer. This mindset limits expansion and keeps you aligned with outdated definitions of what is possible.

Another quiet pattern is the avoidance of closure. Leaving projects unfinished, delaying crucial conversations, or refusing to make final decisions creates a sense of limbo. On the surface, it may seem like caution, but it often masks fear of what success or failure would reveal. By keeping things perpetually "in progress," you avoid confronting the new identity that would come with completion. This pattern can stall careers, relationships, and personal growth for years if left unchecked.

Social dynamics can also play a role. Surrounding yourself with people who reinforce your limitations — whether through subtle criticism, envy, or complacency — can make sabotage feel like loyalty. Choosing growth may mean redefining relationships or setting boundaries that were previously unthinkable. When this discomfort arises, the subconscious sometimes pulls you back into familiar social patterns, even at the cost of your own progress. Awareness of these influences allows you to decide whether your environment supports the life you are building or the one you are leaving behind.

Bringing these patterns to light is not about blaming yourself but about reclaiming power. The moment you identify sabotage, you create a gap between impulse and action. In that space, choice becomes possible. You can pause, question the belief driving the behavior, and decide whether it aligns with your vision. Over time, these small moments of awareness compound into profound shifts. The quiet self-sabotage that once controlled your decisions begins to lose its grip, replaced by intentional actions that support your highest goals.

Practical Release Methods: Clearing Emotional and Mental Clutter

Carrying old emotional baggage is like trying to climb a mountain with unnecessary weight strapped to your back. You may have the strength and the will, but the load slows every step and makes the journey harder than it needs to be. Much of this weight is invisible — unresolved emotions, outdated stories, and mental clutter accumulated over years. Without releasing it, even the most powerful manifestation techniques feel heavy and inconsistent. Clearing this inner clutter is not about erasing the past but about freeing the energy tied up in it so you can use it to create something new.

One of the most effective methods for release is conscious acknowledgment. Many people attempt to bypass uncomfortable feelings, convincing themselves that ignoring pain is the same as healing it. In reality, suppressed emotions stay active in the subconscious, influencing decisions and reactions long after the original event has passed. Bringing these feelings into awareness — naming them without judgment — is the first step toward dissolving their grip. Simply admitting, "I feel resentment," or "I am carrying fear," interrupts the cycle of denial and opens the door to transformation.

Breath-based practices provide another powerful tool. Emotions are stored not only in the mind but in the body, often manifesting as tension in the chest, stomach, or shoulders. Intentional breathing helps unlock these stored patterns. Slow, deep breaths signal safety to the nervous system, allowing previously trapped emotions to surface and release. A simple practice involves inhaling fully, holding for a moment, and exhaling longer than the inhale. This extended exhale activates the body's natural calming response, gradually untangling emotional knots without force.

Writing can serve as both release and clarity. Journaling about unresolved situations or persistent thoughts allows you to externalize what has been circulating internally. The goal is not to craft perfect sentences but to give form to what you feel. A useful exercise is stream-of-consciousness writing: set a timer for ten minutes and write continuously without censoring or editing. This technique bypasses the analytical mind and reveals hidden emotions or beliefs that may otherwise remain buried. Once identified, these insights can be reframed or let go rather than silently directing your choices.

Movement also supports release, particularly when emotions feel too intense for stillness. Physical activity — walking, stretching, dancing — helps process energy that words alone cannot resolve. The body often holds onto experiences that the mind has long forgotten. Shaking out tension, practicing yoga, or even pacing mindfully can shift states quickly, creating space for emotional integration. This is especially effective for people who find traditional meditation challenging because it works with the body's natural impulse to discharge stress rather than suppress it.

Visualization can transform lingering emotional charge into neutrality. By revisiting a memory from a place of safety and imagining it resolving differently, you teach the subconscious that the event no longer defines you. This does not deny what happened but reframes the meaning attached to it. When paired with compassion — offering understanding to the version of yourself who endured it — visualization becomes a bridge between past and present, dissolving the emotional residue left behind.

Forgiveness is another profound yet misunderstood form of release. It is often confused with excusing harmful behavior or denying the impact of past events. In truth, forgiveness is less about the other person and more about reclaiming your own energy. Holding resentment keeps you tethered to the past and continually reactivates emotional wounds. Releasing that attachment does not condone what happened; it simply stops the event from defining your present. A powerful practice involves writing a letter of release — not necessarily to send, but to express every unspoken thought and then symbolically let it go. This act of completion signals to the subconscious that the chapter has closed.

Meditation offers a complementary pathway, especially when combined with mindfulness of emotions as they arise. Rather than trying to silence thoughts, the practice involves witnessing them without identification. When you observe fear, anger, or sadness without immediately reacting, you create space for them to pass naturally. Over time, meditation strengthens your ability to remain steady amid emotional turbulence. This steadiness does not erase challenges but allows you to meet them without being pulled into reactivity, which is itself a form of release.

Ritual can deepen the process for those who resonate with symbolic acts. Human psychology responds strongly to closure marked by physical gestures — burning an old letter, washing hands in water as a symbol of cleansing, or even rearranging a physical space to reflect internal change. These rituals communicate to the subconscious that something has shifted. Because the subconscious responds to sensory experience more than intellectual reasoning, symbolic actions can create a profound sense of resolution that purely mental exercises cannot replicate.

An often-overlooked aspect of clearing emotional clutter is addressing the mental loops that accompany unresolved feelings. Intrusive thoughts about past mistakes or imagined future catastrophes consume energy just as much as heavy emotions do. To break these loops, bring your focus back to what is actually happening in the present moment. Grounding techniques, such as noticing five things you can see, four things you can touch, three things you can hear, two things you can smell, and one thing you can taste, shift attention from rumination to reality. This interrupts the cycle and allows space for clarity to emerge.

Integration is what transforms these practices from temporary relief into lasting change. Releasing once is valuable, but embedding release as an ongoing process creates sustainable freedom. This means checking in with yourself regularly — noticing where tension builds, identifying which thoughts feel heavy, and clearing them before they accumulate. Small, consistent acts of release prevent emotional clutter from returning and keep your mental space open for new possibilities.

The result of consistent release work is not emptiness but lightness. You begin to notice more energy, clearer thinking, and a greater ability to respond to life rather than react to it. Goals that once felt distant become approachable because the weight holding you back is gone. Relationships improve because you are no longer projecting old wounds onto new interactions. Most importantly, you gain a renewed sense of choice. Freed from the grip of old stories, you are able to create new ones — ones that reflect who you are now rather than who you were when those burdens began.

Part III — Quantum Application

Up to this point, you have explored the hidden structures shaping your reality and learned how to realign the inner world that generates them. Understanding energy, subconscious programming, and emotional coherence lays the foundation. But knowledge alone does not create transformation. To embody these principles fully, you must apply them in real time, directly to the moments where life unfolds. This is the leap from theory into practice — the space where ideas become lived experience and reality begins to respond.

Quantum application is not about doing more; it is about doing differently. The principles you have uncovered work in every area of life, but most people apply them sporadically or only when conditions seem perfect. The real power emerges when you integrate them into ordinary moments — when your response to daily challenges becomes an extension of alignment rather than a departure from it. This integration is what turns insight into mastery.

Living this way requires a shift in how you approach both action and perception. Instead of viewing change as something that happens only in structured practices like meditation or journaling, you begin to see every interaction, decision, and challenge as an opportunity to reinforce your chosen frequency. Life stops being divided into "spiritual work" and "real life." The two merge, creating a seamless expression of the identity you are cultivating.

This section explores what it means to live from that place. You will learn how to hold alignment under pressure, respond to chaos without collapsing into fear, and remain receptive to opportunities even when circumstances appear uncertain. The tools here are not abstract concepts but direct practices you can use to navigate relationships, finances, health, and daily challenges. Each one strengthens your ability to stay rooted in the hidden side of reality while engaging fully with the visible world.

The purpose is not perfection but consistency. You will still experience moments of doubt or resistance, but those moments will no longer define you. Instead of being pulled back into old scripts, you will recognize the pattern and return to alignment more quickly. Over time, this consistency compounds. The inner and outer worlds synchronize, and what once felt like effort becomes effortless — a natural extension of who you have become.

By the end of this part, you will not only understand how to work with reality's deeper layers but will be living them as second nature. This is where transformation stops being something you reach for and becomes something you inhabit. It is here, in quantum application, that the hidden side of reality becomes your everyday experience.

Chapter 7: The Structure of Quantum Possibility

Parallel Realities Explained Without the Fluff

The concept of parallel realities has gained popularity in recent years, often wrapped in mystical language or presented as science fiction. In reality, the idea is grounded in both physics and psychology when stripped of exaggeration. Understanding it does not require abandoning reason; it requires expanding how we view choice, perception, and potential. Parallel realities are less about traveling to alternate universes and more about recognizing that countless versions of your life exist as possibilities right now — and that your focus determines which one you experience.

Modern physics offers a lens through which this can be understood. Quantum theory suggests that particles exist in multiple states until observed, a principle known as superposition. When applied metaphorically to human experience, this means your life contains multiple trajectories, each waiting for a point of focus to collapse it into reality. At any moment, countless outcomes are possible: a relationship succeeding or ending, a career thriving or stagnating, health improving or declining. Your choices and, more importantly, your consistent patterns of thought and emotion determine which outcome becomes tangible.

This does not imply that every imagined scenario instantly exists in the same way physical matter does. Rather, it acknowledges that potential outcomes coexist until energy and focus stabilize one path. In simpler terms, reality responds to where you invest your attention and how you align your actions with that focus. If you habitually focus on scarcity, you reinforce the version of life where scarcity dominates. Shift focus toward abundance and embody that perspective consistently, and you activate the version of reality where abundance is available.

Parallel realities also explain why transformation can feel sudden from the outside. People sometimes describe breakthroughs as if "everything changed overnight." In truth, their external circumstances often shift rapidly after an internal threshold is crossed. The moment their identity, beliefs, and emotions align with a new outcome, they effectively step into a different version of life that was always available but previously inaccessible to them. From the inside, it feels like gradual inner work. From the outside, it looks like a sudden leap.

This framework eliminates the myth that change must take years or follow a linear path. Growth can be incremental, but it can also be quantum — meaning it happens in leaps rather than steps. When alignment reaches a tipping point, the shift feels instantaneous. The key is not in forcing the leap but in preparing for it: clearing resistance, aligning emotion with intention, and acting in congruence with the version of yourself you intend to become.

The practicality of this concept lies in its application. Recognizing parallel realities is useless if it remains theoretical. The real value comes from using it to guide daily choices. If every moment contains access to countless potential outcomes, the question becomes: which reality are you feeding with your attention? Each decision — from how you respond to challenges to what you imagine when you think about your future — reinforces one version of life over another. Awareness of this power brings responsibility but also liberation.

Understanding this concept also reframes failure and setbacks. Instead of seeing them as fixed outcomes, you begin to view them as indicators of which reality you are currently aligned with. This shift in perspective removes the heaviness from mistakes. A misstep is not the end of the story; it is a sign that you are reinforcing an older pattern and an invitation to redirect. When you realize you can always shift alignment, failure loses its permanence and becomes part of the refinement process.

A key factor in this process is emotional congruence. Thoughts may set direction, but emotions determine whether the subconscious accepts the new trajectory as real. Someone can visualize success while feeling unworthy of it, unintentionally feeding the reality where success remains distant. By aligning emotional states with chosen outcomes, you signal to both your nervous system and the environment that this version of reality is safe and familiar. This is why cultivating elevated states such as trust, gratitude, or calmness is essential — they bridge the gap between potential and manifestation.

Behavior is the final reinforcement. Parallel realities are not just about thought and feeling but about action that matches the identity you are stepping into. When your choices reflect the life you intend to live, you confirm that reality to yourself repeatedly. These do not have to be dramatic actions; even small decisions, like how you start your morning or how you respond to discomfort, carry weight. Over time, these micro-actions accumulate and stabilize the shift into a different life trajectory.

It is also worth acknowledging that this process is not instant, even though quantum leaps are possible. The subconscious requires evidence to fully adopt a new identity. At first, this evidence may come from imagination and emotional rehearsal. Eventually, it emerges through consistent behavior and subtle changes in external circumstances. Patience here is not passive waiting; it is active participation in the gradual synchronization of inner and outer worlds.

Skepticism is natural when encountering this framework, especially for those who prefer concrete explanations. Rather than dismissing skepticism, use it to refine your understanding. The concept of parallel realities does not require belief in infinite universes or fantastical timelines; it is about recognizing how choice and perception continuously shape experience. By grounding the principle in observable shifts — how focus changes behavior, how behavior influences results — it becomes practical rather than abstract. Living with this awareness transforms everyday decisions. Choosing how you respond to a challenge is no longer just about coping; it is about deciding which version of reality you are stepping into. Each moment offers a chance to reinforce the past or align with a new future. The more you treat these decisions as conscious opportunities, the more fluid life feels. External change stops being mysterious and starts to feel like a natural consequence of internal alignment.

Ultimately, parallel realities are not about escape but about access. The life you want does not exist in some distant dimension; it is available in this moment, waiting for you to align with it. The work is not in chasing it down but in becoming the version of yourself who naturally inhabits it. Once that shift occurs, what once seemed impossible begins to unfold as if it were always meant to happen.

Navigating Probabilities: Why Every Choice Creates a Fork

Life unfolds as a series of choices, many so small they barely register at the moment they are made. Whether you answer a phone call, take a different route home, or decide to speak your mind in a meeting, each decision influences what becomes possible next. From this perspective, reality is not fixed but branching — a network of probabilities continuously shifting based on where you place your attention and how you act.

Understanding this branching nature of reality does not require mystical thinking. It reflects a principle visible in both human behavior and physics: cause and effect are not linear but layered. A single decision rarely determines everything, but it initiates a cascade of changes. What you say yes or no to determines which doors remain open and which quietly close. Over time, the accumulation of these forks creates entirely different trajectories — not just in circumstances but in identity.

One way to grasp this is to consider how small choices compound over time. Choosing to engage in a daily habit, like consistent exercise or journaling, might seem insignificant on any single day. But each repetition reinforces a particular version of reality: one where discipline and growth are normal. Conversely, avoiding these small commitments reinforces a version where stagnation feels inevitable. These diverging paths begin subtly but become strikingly different months or years later.

This framework also clarifies why people can share similar external conditions yet experience vastly different outcomes. Two individuals may grow up in comparable environments, but their responses to daily forks — who they spend time with, what opportunities they pursue, how they interpret setbacks — lead to divergent lives. The difference is not just external luck; it is the cumulative effect of choices interacting with probabilities.

Every fork carries both visible and invisible consequences. Some outcomes are immediate and tangible, like the results of a conversation or a financial decision. Others are subtler, influencing mindset and belief systems. Saying no to an opportunity out of fear, for example, may not only close that specific door but also reinforce an internal story of limitation. Over time, these reinforced beliefs shape future choices, creating a feedback loop that either expands or contracts your sense of possibility.

Navigating this landscape begins with awareness. Most choices are made automatically, guided by subconscious programming rather than deliberate intention. Recognizing that every decision contributes to a larger trajectory encourages greater presence. It invites you to pause and ask: Does this choice align with the reality I want to create? Even when the decision seems trivial, the cumulative effect of aligned micro-choices is profound.

This understanding also reframes responsibility. If reality is shaped by probabilities, then nothing is entirely predetermined, but neither is it random. The future is not a single path waiting to be discovered; it is a field of options responding to your participation. This awareness can feel both empowering and intimidating. Empowering, because it means you are not trapped by past choices; intimidating, because it removes the comfort of blaming chance.

Seeing life as a series of forks does not mean overanalyzing every move or fearing mistakes. It is about cultivating discernment without falling into perfectionism. The truth is that not every choice needs to be monumental. What matters is the general trajectory your repeated decisions create. A single decision rarely defines you, but repeated patterns do. Choosing alignment once is powerful; choosing it consistently creates momentum strong enough to shift the entire probability field in your favor.

This awareness naturally changes how you approach setbacks. Instead of believing one poor decision ruins everything, you recognize it as a single branch in a much larger tree of possibilities. The moment you become aware of misalignment, you can redirect. Each fork offers another chance to choose differently. This perspective removes the pressure of perfection and replaces it with an ongoing dialogue: Who am I choosing to be now?

The power of choice also lies in how you interpret circumstances. Two people can face the same external event — a job loss, a failed project, a difficult conversation — and walk away with entirely different trajectories because of the meaning they assign to it. One may view it as proof of inadequacy and spiral into avoidance, while the other interprets it as an opening to realign and pursue something better. The fork was not in the event itself but in the story told about it.

Cultivating this level of awareness begins by slowing down. Pausing before automatic responses creates room for new possibilities. When you notice yourself about to repeat an old pattern — dismissing an idea, withdrawing from discomfort, saying yes out of obligation — that pause is a doorway. Even a brief moment of reflection disrupts the automatic loop and reintroduces choice. Over time, these interruptions weaken the old pathways and strengthen new ones.

An essential aspect of navigating probabilities is clarity about your desired trajectory. Without a clear sense of where you are heading, it is easy to drift between branches without intention. Clarity does not require knowing every detail of the future; it requires knowing the quality of experience you are moving toward. Do you want peace or chaos? Expansion or contraction? Freedom or security at all costs? Once these qualities are defined, they serve as a compass for the daily micro-decisions that shape your life.

This understanding does not eliminate uncertainty. Probability, by definition, leaves room for unpredictability. Unexpected events will still arise, but awareness shifts how you respond. Instead of being thrown off course, you use them as information: Do I adjust my approach, or do I hold my direction despite temporary turbulence? Life becomes less about control and more about alignment with chosen principles, regardless of external fluctuations.

Over time, this way of navigating life produces visible shifts. Opportunities that once seemed rare become frequent because your decisions naturally lead you into environments where they exist. Relationships feel more intentional because you choose them rather than stumble into them. Progress feels less like forcing outcomes and more like flowing toward them. The forks never stop appearing, but your relationship to them transforms. You no longer fear them; you welcome them as invitations to create, moment by moment, the reality you are ready to live.

How to "Shift Timelines" With Intentional Action and Awareness

The idea of shifting timelines can sound abstract, but when stripped of mystical language, it simply refers to creating a profound change in trajectory through conscious awareness and deliberate choice. Rather than drifting along the default path created by old conditioning, you learn to intentionally step into a version of reality that aligns with your highest vision. This process is less about forcing outcomes and more about embodying a different state of being that naturally draws those outcomes to you.

At its core, shifting timelines begins with awareness of where you currently stand. Most people move through life reacting to circumstances without questioning whether those circumstances reflect outdated beliefs. They interpret the present as fixed rather than as a snapshot of past choices and emotional patterns. The first step is to recognize that what you experience today is not inevitable but the result of alignment with a particular probability. This recognition alone dissolves the feeling of being trapped and opens the possibility for change.

Intentional action comes next. Awareness without application leaves the old trajectory intact. To shift timelines, every decision must begin to reflect the identity you are moving toward, even before external evidence supports it. This is where many people struggle, because the mind demands proof before committing. Yet waiting for proof keeps you aligned with the old version of reality. The shift occurs when you act as if the new version is already true, not as a performance but as a genuine choice about who you are becoming.

This approach requires a balance of inner and outer work. Internally, you cultivate emotional coherence — ensuring your feelings support your intentions rather than contradict them. If you want abundance but consistently feel fear or scarcity, those emotions anchor you to the old timeline. By practicing gratitude, presence, and self-trust, you raise your emotional state to match the reality you wish to inhabit. Externally, you follow through with aligned action. This may mean making different financial decisions, changing how you communicate in relationships, or setting new boundaries that reflect your evolving values.

Clarity about your desired timeline is essential. You do not need to map every detail, but you must define the essence of the reality you are choosing. Is it freedom? Peace? Creative fulfillment? Once this essence is clear, you can evaluate every choice against it: Does this move me closer to or further from that reality? This simple question turns everyday decisions into powerful moments of alignment.

Shifting timelines also involves releasing attachment to how the change unfolds. Many people attempt to control every variable, which ironically keeps them stuck. The more you try to force a specific path, the more you reinforce the belief that the new reality is out of reach. The key is to focus on embodying the state that matches your desired outcome while remaining flexible about the form it takes. Opportunities often arise in ways the rational mind could not predict, and staying open allows you to recognize them when they appear.

Consistency is what anchors the new timeline. A single act of alignment can spark change, but sustained repetition rewires identity. Each time you respond differently than you would have in the past — choosing patience over reactivity, courage over avoidance, or trust over fear — you strengthen the neural and emotional pathways associated with the new reality. Eventually, these choices become automatic. The version of you who once struggled to believe in new possibilities is replaced by the version who lives them effortlessly.

This process is rarely linear. Old patterns may resurface, and external circumstances might temporarily reflect the past even as you shift internally. These moments are not signs of failure but opportunities to reaffirm your direction. When setbacks occur, the question becomes: Do you react as the old self or respond as the new one? Each reaffirmation deepens your alignment and signals to the subconscious that the new timeline is stable.

Another key element is cultivating an internal sense of safety during change. The subconscious resists unfamiliar experiences because it equates the unknown with danger. By creating practices that regulate your nervous system — mindful breathing, grounding, or even simple routines that anchor you — you teach the body that transformation is safe. This reduces internal resistance and allows shifts to happen with less friction.

Supporting environments amplify the process. Surrounding yourself with people, spaces, and information that reflect your chosen reality reinforces the shift. This is not about perfection in external conditions but about curating influences that make it easier to stay aligned. If you are seeking peace, exposure to constant chaos will slow the process. If you are cultivating abundance, immersing yourself in conversations of lack will conflict with your focus. Adjusting your environment ensures that internal changes are not constantly undermined by external signals.

Patience and trust are crucial. Timeline shifts often feel subtle until they suddenly become obvious. For weeks or months, progress may seem invisible, then a single event reveals how much has changed — an opportunity arises, a habit no longer feels forced, or a relationship transforms. These breakthroughs are the visible result of countless unseen micro-choices. Trusting the process keeps you from abandoning it too early, especially in the quiet phases where results have not yet manifested.

Ultimately, shifting timelines is not about escaping your current life but about engaging it differently. The external world may look similar at first, but your experience of it transforms as your perception and behavior change. This is why people who undergo profound inner shifts often describe their life as "the same, yet completely different." The external circumstances did not magically vanish; their relationship to those circumstances evolved, allowing new pathways to emerge.

When practiced consistently, intentional awareness and aligned action turn timeline shifting from an occasional breakthrough into a way of living. You stop waiting for life to change and begin participating in its unfolding. Every choice becomes a vote for the reality you wish to inhabit, and over time those votes accumulate into something undeniable. The shift feels less like magic and more like inevitability — the natural result of becoming fully congruent with the life you were meant to experience.

Chapter 8: Aligning Desire With Purpose

Why Manifestation Fails Without True Alignment

Many people approach manifestation as if it were a single-step process: think about what you want, visualize it, and wait for it to appear. While intention is a critical element, it is only one part of the equation. Without alignment — the harmony of thought, emotion, belief, and action — even the clearest vision can remain out of reach. This is why so many people feel frustrated when manifestation "does not work" for them. They are focusing on the surface while ignoring the deeper structures that either allow or block what they desire.

Alignment is often misunderstood as merely "positive thinking." In reality, alignment requires coherence between multiple layers of your inner world. You might consciously affirm abundance, yet subconsciously fear it. You may visualize love while secretly believing you are unworthy of it. These inner contradictions split your energy. The conscious mind sends one message, while the subconscious sends another, and the result is confusion rather than creation.

The subconscious is especially powerful because it governs most of your behavior automatically. Even if you set a conscious intention for success, old patterns rooted in fear or scarcity can override it. This is why repeating affirmations without addressing underlying beliefs often feels hollow. True alignment involves identifying and transforming the deeper scripts that dictate how you perceive yourself and the world. Until this happens, your external actions will unconsciously reinforce the very reality you are trying to escape.

Emotion is another critical factor. Manifestation is not purely intellectual; it is vibrational. The emotions you habitually embody shape the signal you broadcast. Wanting something from a place of lack tends to perpetuate lack, because the focus is still on the absence rather than the fulfillment. This does not mean you must feel joyful every moment, but it does mean you must learn to cultivate states of trust, openness, and gratitude even before evidence appears. Emotions are the bridge between thought and reality, and they determine how effectively your intentions take root.

Action is the final layer of alignment. Many people treat manifestation as a passive process, waiting for the universe to deliver without participation. But aligned action is not about frantic effort; it is about congruence. When you take steps that match the identity you are cultivating, you reinforce to yourself and to the world that you are ready for what you desire. This could mean setting boundaries, saying yes to opportunities, or investing in personal growth. The actions may be small, but they carry weight because they reflect a shift in identity.

Without this harmony of belief, emotion, and action, even the most vivid visualizations can feel ineffective. People often interpret this as evidence that manifestation "does not work," when in truth it is a signal that deeper alignment is needed. Once the internal conflict is resolved, results often appear quickly, not because they suddenly became possible, but because nothing is resisting them anymore.

A crucial part of achieving alignment is noticing where resistance hides. Often, it shows up in subtle ways — procrastination, self-sabotage, or constant second-guessing. These behaviors are not signs of laziness but indicators of misaligned beliefs. When your subconscious is not on board with your conscious goals, it creates friction that slows progress. Identifying these patterns allows you to address them directly instead of blaming external circumstances.

The process of bringing subconscious beliefs into harmony with conscious intention begins with honest self-inquiry. Asking questions like "Do I actually believe this is possible for me?" or "What part of me doubts this outcome?" exposes hidden conflicts. These questions may surface uncomfortable truths — memories of past failures, fears of judgment, or inherited messages about what is "realistic." Confronting them is not always easy, but it is necessary. Without acknowledging them, you risk layering affirmations on top of unresolved fear, which only creates tension.

Another overlooked aspect of alignment is readiness to receive. Many people hold visions of what they want but feel uneasy about what having it would actually require. Wanting financial freedom, for example, might also mean being visible, making larger decisions, or taking on new responsibilities. If you secretly feel unsafe with those possibilities, you unconsciously block them. True alignment includes preparing emotionally and mentally for the life you are calling in so that when opportunities arrive, you are willing to embrace them.

Embodiment is the bridge that closes the gap between intention and reality. It is not enough to think about who you want to become; you must begin to live as that version now. This does not mean faking confidence or pretending circumstances are different than they are. It means making daily choices that reflect the identity you are stepping into — speaking with integrity, caring for your body, setting boundaries, and prioritizing actions that support your vision. Over time, these choices solidify the new identity until it feels natural rather than aspirational.

Patience is also integral to alignment. Many people abandon the process too early because they expect instant results. When external conditions do not shift right away, they assume nothing is happening. In reality, alignment often begins as an internal recalibration long before visible evidence appears. The nervous system learns to trust the new reality, old habits dissolve, and emotional responses evolve. Once this foundation is secure, external changes tend to unfold rapidly. Recognizing this rhythm prevents frustration and keeps you committed during quieter phases.

Ultimately, alignment is about integrity — not in the moral sense, but in the structural sense of wholeness. When thoughts, emotions, and actions point in the same direction, energy flows without obstruction. You stop sending mixed signals and begin broadcasting a clear message to both yourself and the world. This is the state in which manifestation feels less like effort and more like resonance. Opportunities seem to "find" you because you are finally in harmony with them.

When people say manifestation works "like magic," what they are describing is the experience of true alignment. It feels magical because it bypasses struggle, yet it is grounded in principles that are repeatable and practical. By resolving internal conflicts, embodying the desired identity, and taking aligned action, you turn vague hopes into lived reality. Alignment is not an optional extra to manifestation; it is the mechanism that makes it work.

The Difference Between Ego Desires and Soul Desires

Not every desire we hold is created equal. Some emerge from the deeper essence of who we are, calling us toward growth, fulfillment, and alignment with our true nature. Others arise from fear, insecurity, or a craving for validation — a drive to prove something rather than live something. Understanding the difference between ego desires and soul desires is crucial because chasing the wrong kind of desire can lead to temporary satisfaction but long-term emptiness. True transformation and lasting manifestation only happen when the goals you pursue reflect the deeper call of your soul. Ego desires are rooted in the part of you that is concerned with identity and survival. The ego seeks safety, approval, and control. It wants to avoid pain and gain advantage in ways that make it feel significant. This is not inherently bad; the ego plays a role in navigating everyday life. But when unexamined, ego-driven desires tend to be reactive rather than authentic. They emerge as responses to perceived lack: wanting success to silence feelings of inadequacy, craving recognition to mask feelings of invisibility, or seeking wealth to prove worthiness.

These desires often carry a frantic energy. They feel urgent, as if achieving them will finally bring relief from discomfort. Yet when they are fulfilled, the satisfaction rarely lasts. You may achieve the external milestone — the job title, the relationship, the financial target — only to find yourself asking, "Is this it?" The underlying hunger remains because the desire was never about the thing itself; it was about filling an inner void. Without addressing the void, no amount of accomplishment will feel complete.

Soul desires, by contrast, arise from a deeper intelligence. They are less about proving something and more about expressing something already true. Instead of seeking validation, they invite expansion. A soul desire might call you toward creative work, deeper connection, or service to others — not because you lack worth, but because it feels aligned with who you already are. Pursuing these desires often brings a sense of peace, even in the midst of effort, because they resonate with your natural values and strengths.

The quality of energy around soul desires is quieter yet more persistent. They may not feel as urgent as ego-driven goals, but they do not fade with time. A dream that keeps resurfacing despite fear or practicality is often a signal from the soul. Following it tends to create a sense of harmony rather than tension. Even when challenges arise, there is meaning in the process because the journey itself feels aligned.

Recognizing the difference between these two types of desires requires deep honesty. It is not always obvious which is driving you because ego and soul can want similar things for very different reasons. Both might desire financial abundance, for example, but ego seeks it to escape fear while soul seeks it to create freedom and contribute meaningfully. The external goal may look identical, yet the internal motivation transforms the experience of pursuing and receiving it.

One of the clearest indicators of an ego-driven desire is how it feels when progress is delayed or recognition does not arrive. The ego becomes restless, impatient, or resentful when its efforts are not validated by quick results. This reaction exposes its underlying motive: a search for external confirmation of worth. Soul desires, on the other hand, remain steady even in uncertainty. There may be moments of doubt, but the desire itself does not vanish under pressure. Instead, it grows stronger, inviting you to trust the process rather than control the outcome.

Another way to distinguish them is to examine how the desire influences your relationship with yourself and others. Ego desires often foster comparison and competition. They thrive on being better than, ahead of, or more than someone else. Soul desires inspire collaboration and authenticity. They encourage you to share your gifts rather than hoard them, to celebrate others' successes rather than feel threatened by them. When pursuing a soul desire, you feel expanded rather than contracted.

Listening to your body can also provide insight. Ego desires often create tension — a tightening in the chest, a sense of striving or pushing. Soul desires bring a sense of grounded excitement or quiet clarity. Even if the path ahead is uncertain, there is an inner knowing that the pursuit is right. This somatic feedback is subtle but reliable, especially when combined with honest reflection on your motives.

To align with soul desires, it helps to slow down and question your goals. Ask why you want what you want, and then ask why again. Often the first answer reveals surface reasoning, while deeper layers uncover true motives. If the desire is about avoiding fear or proving worth, it may be ego-driven. If it is about expression, contribution, or fulfillment regardless of external validation, it likely originates from the soul. This inquiry is not about shaming ego-based desires but about discerning which ones truly lead to lasting satisfaction.

Integrating this awareness into daily life requires humility and patience. The ego is loud and reactive; the soul is quiet and persistent. Creating space to hear that quieter voice means cultivating stillness — through meditation, journaling, or time in nature — so that clarity can emerge without interference from constant noise. Over time, you begin to recognize the subtle difference between impulsive cravings and enduring callings.

When you align with soul desires, manifestation feels different. Instead of chasing outcomes, you embody them. Instead of forcing circumstances, you flow with them. Life begins to feel less like climbing a ladder and more like stepping into a current that already knows where it is going. This does not mean there are no challenges, but the challenges feel purposeful rather than punishing. The journey itself becomes part of the fulfillment, not just the means to an end.

Ultimately, distinguishing between ego and soul is about returning to authenticity. The ego asks, "What will make me look worthy?" The soul asks, "What feels true to me?" When you build your life around the latter question, fulfillment is not something you chase; it is something you live.

Practical Steps to Clarify Your Authentic Vision

Clarity is the foundation of any meaningful transformation. Without it, you may pour energy into goals that do not truly belong to you or chase outcomes that fail to satisfy once achieved. Authentic vision emerges when you peel back the layers of expectation — from family, culture, or even your own past self — and discover what your deeper nature is asking for now. This process is not about predicting every detail of the future but about uncovering the essence of the life you want to create.

The first step in clarifying vision is quieting external noise. Constant input from social media, advertising, and comparison distorts your sense of what matters. When everyone is broadcasting curated images of success, it is easy to adopt desires that are not your own. Setting aside intentional time for silence and reflection helps separate genuine inspiration from borrowed aspirations. This does not require withdrawing from life but does require conscious boundaries — moments without screens, spaces free of distraction, and deliberate pauses to reconnect with yourself.

Once external noise is quieted, self-inquiry becomes possible. Begin by asking simple yet profound questions: "What experiences make me feel most alive?" "When do I feel at peace with myself?" "If nothing were impossible and no one would judge me, what would I choose?" Write down your responses without censoring them. The purpose is not immediate perfection but uncovering patterns. Over time, recurring themes reveal values and desires that persist beyond fleeting trends or temporary emotions.

Another powerful approach is examining contrast. Clarity often arises not only from knowing what you want but from recognizing what you no longer wish to tolerate. Reflect on moments of frustration, exhaustion, or dissatisfaction in your life. What do these experiences reveal about what you are ready to release? Identifying what feels misaligned creates space to define what alignment would look like. For example, recognizing that constant busyness drains you may illuminate a deeper desire for simplicity or creative freedom.

Visualization can deepen this process when used intentionally. Rather than imagining only external achievements, focus on how you want to feel in your future life. Picture yourself waking up in alignment: What is the tone of your day? How do your surroundings reflect your values? Who are you becoming as you live this way? Emotional detail matters because the subconscious responds strongly to feeling. When you can sense the peace, excitement, or fulfillment of your authentic vision, it becomes easier to recognize when choices align with it.

Clarifying vision also involves questioning inherited narratives about success. Many people pursue goals handed down by family or culture — a certain career path, income level, or lifestyle — without examining whether those goals bring meaning. Ask yourself whose definition of success you are living by. If the answer feels disconnected from your own inner truth, it is time to rewrite that definition. True vision does not arise from obligation; it arises from resonance.

One of the most effective ways to refine your vision is to connect it with your core values. Values act as a compass, guiding decisions even when external circumstances change. Begin by identifying the qualities you want your life to reflect — freedom, growth, creativity, connection, or contribution. When a vision aligns with these core principles, it tends to endure rather than shift with trends or fleeting emotions. If a goal does not resonate with your deeper values, it may create short-term excitement but long-term dissonance.

After identifying values, translate them into tangible expressions. If freedom is a value, what does that look like in daily life? Is it location independence, financial flexibility, or freedom of time? If connection is important, does it mean building deep personal relationships, serving a community, or collaborating on meaningful work? This translation turns abstract ideals into actionable direction. Without this step, values remain inspiring but vague, which makes it difficult to create aligned plans.

Another crucial element is acknowledging fear and doubt without letting them dictate vision. Many people unconsciously lower their goals to avoid disappointment. They settle for what seems "realistic" rather than what feels true. This cautious approach might protect from short-term risk but guarantees long-term regret. Instead of suppressing fear, observe it and ask whether it signals genuine misalignment or simply the discomfort of expansion. Often, fear arises not because the vision is wrong but because it stretches beyond familiar limits.

Clarity also grows through experimentation. Waiting for perfect certainty before acting creates paralysis. Taking small steps toward a possible vision

— trying a new skill, joining a community, or rearranging your schedule — provides feedback you cannot gain through thought alone. These experiments reveal what energizes you, what drains you, and where adjustments are needed. Over time, they transform abstract ideas into lived insights and help refine your path with greater precision.

Journaling remains one of the most practical tools for this process. Writing bypasses the filters of the conscious mind, allowing hidden truths to surface. You can use prompts such as, "If I fully trusted myself, what would I create?" or "What part of me have I been ignoring?" Reviewing your entries over time highlights patterns and recurring desires that point to your authentic vision. Unlike fleeting inspiration, these patterns remain steady and reliable markers of alignment.

Finally, clarifying vision is not a one-time event but an ongoing dialogue with yourself. As you evolve, so will your desires. What felt aligned five years ago may not reflect who you are today. This does not mean past visions were wrong; it means you have grown. Periodically revisiting and refining your vision ensures it continues to reflect your current truth rather than outdated versions of yourself. Staying open to evolution keeps your goals alive and prevents the stagnation that comes from rigid expectations.

When clarity is reached, there is a noticeable shift in energy. Doubt does not vanish, but direction emerges. Decision-making becomes simpler because you know what you are moving toward. This sense of inner alignment fuels persistence through challenges and creates a quiet confidence that no external approval can replicate. With vision clarified, every choice — large or small — becomes an opportunity to step more fully into the life that already resonates within you.

Chapter 9: Applying the Framework to Key Life Areas

Rewiring Your Relationship With Money and Abundance

For many people, money is one of the most emotionally charged topics in life. It represents survival, freedom, security, and possibility — yet it also carries layers of fear, shame, and inherited beliefs. These beliefs often form long before we are aware of them, shaped by childhood experiences, cultural narratives, and family dynamics. Without consciously addressing them, they create invisible limits on what we feel capable of receiving and holding. To truly experience abundance, the relationship with money itself must be rewired.

The first step in this rewiring is uncovering the hidden stories you carry about money. Many of these narratives are subtle yet powerful: "Money is hard to earn," "Rich people are greedy," or "I am not good with finances." These beliefs operate beneath conscious thought, influencing decisions and emotional responses. For example, someone who believes wealth is corrupting may unconsciously sabotage opportunities for financial growth to preserve a sense of morality. Another person who believes money is scarce might hoard it anxiously, never feeling safe no matter how much they accumulate.

Identifying these narratives requires honest reflection. Think back to the messages you absorbed in childhood: How did your family talk about money? Was it a source of conflict, pride, secrecy, or security? What emotions surfaced when money was discussed? These early impressions often become default programming, quietly shaping how you relate to finances as an adult. Recognizing them is not about blaming your past but about reclaiming the power to choose new beliefs that serve you now.

Once these stories are visible, the next step is reframing them. Reframing does not mean ignoring reality or pretending challenges do not exist; it means questioning whether your current beliefs are absolute truths or simply inherited perspectives. Consider the belief "Money is hard to earn." Is this universally true, or are there people who earn money with ease and joy? If exceptions exist, then the belief is not a law of nature but a perspective you can shift. This opens the door to adopting a more empowering narrative, such as "Money flows to me as I create value" or "I am capable of learning the skills to manage and grow wealth."

Equally important is redefining what abundance means to you personally. Many people chase numbers without considering the deeper experience they seek — freedom, security, the ability to give generously, or time to pursue meaningful work. When abundance is reduced to a dollar amount, it often creates endless striving. By connecting money to values and desired experiences, you create a more holistic and fulfilling relationship with it. This shift reduces pressure and fosters gratitude for the abundance already present in non-monetary forms, such as relationships, health, and opportunities.

Healing the emotional charge around money is another vital step. Guilt about having too much, shame about not having enough, or anxiety about losing what you have can keep you in a cycle of scarcity even during financial growth. Practices like journaling, somatic release, or guided visualization can help neutralize these emotions. When money no longer triggers survival-level stress, it becomes easier to make clear, aligned financial decisions rather than reactive ones rooted in fear.

Cultivating a mindset of sufficiency is one of the most transformative practices you can adopt. Sufficiency does not mean complacency or giving up on growth; it means recognizing that you are not starting from lack. When you begin with gratitude for what you already have, your decisions are no longer made from desperation but from grounded clarity. This shift opens space for expansion without the constant pressure of "never enough" that drives many people into burnout or reckless financial choices.

Practical alignment with abundance requires consistent behaviors that reflect trust in your evolving narrative about money. This might include mindful budgeting that prioritizes both present needs and future goals, or setting aside a portion of income for experiences that nourish your sense of joy rather than only for obligations. Small, repeated actions like paying bills with appreciation rather than resentment or consciously celebrating every inflow of money — no matter the amount — retrain the nervous system to associate finances with safety rather than threat.

Equally vital is dismantling the belief that wealth and spirituality or personal integrity cannot coexist. This false dichotomy often prevents people from fully receiving abundance, as if financial success automatically means abandoning deeper values. In truth, money amplifies who you already are. When aligned with purpose, it becomes a tool for contribution, freedom, and impact. Shifting this belief allows you to approach wealth creation not as a compromise of values but as an extension of them.

Integrating generosity into your financial framework accelerates this rewiring. Generosity signals trust in ongoing flow rather than fear of depletion. It does not have to be grand; even small acts of giving — offering time, resources, or support — reinforce a sense of abundance and interconnectedness. The act of giving shifts focus from scarcity to contribution, which strengthens the belief that you are part of a larger cycle of exchange rather than isolated struggle.

As your internal relationship with money evolves, external opportunities often begin to align in surprising ways. You may notice doors opening that once seemed closed or creative solutions emerging to challenges that felt insurmountable. This is not coincidence but a reflection of new patterns: when you release fear and reframe beliefs, you make choices that previously felt impossible. Over time, these choices compound into tangible shifts in income, savings, and lifestyle — changes that feel earned yet almost effortless because they emerge from congruence rather than force.

The work of rewiring does not end with a single breakthrough. Old patterns can resurface during periods of stress or transition, which is why ongoing awareness is essential. Regularly revisiting your beliefs, practicing gratitude, and aligning financial choices with your core values ensures that new habits become deeply rooted rather than temporary. This approach transforms money from a source of tension into a neutral or even uplifting presence in your life, freeing energy for creativity, relationships, and purpose.

When your relationship with money reflects trust, clarity, and alignment, abundance stops being something you chase and becomes something you live. You no longer view wealth as distant or conditional but as a natural byproduct of living authentically and creating value. This is the foundation for not only financial growth but also a deeper sense of peace — the knowing that you can meet life's demands while continuing to expand into greater possibilities.

Transforming Relationships Through Inner Alignment

Relationships often mirror the state of our inner world more than we realize. The patterns we experience with others — whether harmonious or conflicted — frequently reflect beliefs, emotions, and expectations we carry within ourselves. This is why similar issues can arise across different relationships, even when the people involved are completely different. Transforming relationships at the deepest level begins not with changing others but with aligning the self.

When you approach relationships from inner misalignment, unconscious needs and fears often drive behavior. You might seek validation rather than connection, control rather than trust, or approval rather than authenticity. This can create cycles of disappointment, as no amount of external reassurance resolves the internal void fueling the dynamic. The relationship becomes a stage where unhealed wounds are acted out rather than healed. Without conscious awareness, these patterns repeat across partners, friends, colleagues, or even family members.

Inner alignment changes this dynamic. When your sense of worth no longer depends on external validation, you approach relationships with more openness and less defensiveness. You are able to listen without immediately taking things personally, set boundaries without guilt, and give love without expecting it to fill unmet needs. This shift creates space for healthier interactions, where both people are free to be authentic rather than performing roles to meet each other's insecurities.

A key part of this transformation is identifying the beliefs you hold about relationships themselves. Many people unconsciously adopt narratives like "love always ends in pain," "people cannot be trusted," or "I have to earn affection." These beliefs shape expectations and behaviors in subtle ways, often creating self-fulfilling prophecies. By bringing these assumptions into awareness, you can challenge and replace them with beliefs that support deeper connection and respect.

Emotional regulation is another essential element. Relationships inevitably bring moments of tension or misunderstanding. Without alignment, these moments can trigger disproportionate reactions — anger, withdrawal, or anxiety — rooted in old wounds rather than the present situation. Learning to pause, breathe, and observe emotions before reacting allows you to respond intentionally instead of habitually. This not only prevents escalation but also fosters trust, as others sense the stability you bring to the interaction.

Alignment also involves clarifying what you truly value in relationships. Many people seek connection without defining what kind of connection they desire. Do you value mutual growth, emotional intimacy, shared purpose, or freedom within partnership? Understanding these priorities prevents you from accepting dynamics that do not serve you simply out of habit or fear of loneliness. It also helps you recognize when a relationship is aligned and worth nurturing, versus when it consistently violates your core values.

This process does not only apply to romantic relationships. Inner alignment improves interactions across all areas of life — friendships, family, professional connections, and even brief encounters with strangers. As you shift internally, the energy you project changes, often inviting different responses from others without needing to demand or force it. People sense when someone is grounded and authentic, and they naturally feel safer and more open in that presence.

Healing past relational wounds plays a crucial role in sustaining this alignment. Many triggers in present-day interactions stem from unresolved experiences, such as childhood abandonment, betrayal in previous partnerships, or patterns learned from observing caregivers. When these memories remain unprocessed, the nervous system reacts to present situations as though the past were repeating itself. Recognizing when you are reacting to an old wound rather than the current moment allows you to separate past pain from present reality, which is the first step toward transforming the way you relate to others.

This process of healing does not always require the other person to change. Often, the transformation begins internally through self-forgiveness and compassion. Acknowledging your own part in past patterns — without blame or shame — frees you to create healthier dynamics moving forward. As you soften toward yourself, it becomes easier to extend that same compassion to others, even when boundaries are necessary.

Boundaries themselves are a vital component of aligned relationships. Contrary to the belief that boundaries push people away, they actually create the safety necessary for closeness. When your limits are clear and honored, resentment diminishes and authentic connection flourishes.

Communicating boundaries calmly and consistently prevents misunderstandings and ensures that relationships grow from mutual respect rather than unspoken expectations.

As alignment deepens, you also develop the ability to discern which relationships are worth investing in. Not every connection is meant to last, and inner clarity makes it easier to release relationships that are chronically misaligned without unnecessary guilt. This is not an act of rejection but of honoring both parties' growth. When you stop clinging to connections that drain you, you create space for relationships that nourish you.

Another profound shift occurs in how you give and receive love. Without alignment, love can feel transactional — given to get something in return. With alignment, love flows more freely because it is not dependent on conditions. You appreciate others for who they are rather than what they provide. This shift transforms even difficult relationships, as your responses are no longer dictated by fear of loss or need for control but by a steady sense of inner wholeness.

Alignment also enhances your ability to navigate conflict. Rather than viewing disagreements as threats, you begin to see them as opportunities for deeper understanding. The focus shifts from winning an argument to uncovering the truth beneath the tension — unmet needs, unspoken fears, or differing values. Approaching conflict with curiosity rather than defensiveness fosters repair and strengthens trust, even when solutions are not immediate.

The ripple effects of this transformation extend far beyond personal satisfaction. When you operate from alignment, you naturally model a different way of relating. Others may feel inspired to reflect on their own patterns and make changes in response. Over time, your personal growth contributes to healthier dynamics in families, workplaces, and communities. Change at the individual level becomes change at the collective level, one aligned relationship at a time.

Ultimately, transforming relationships through inner alignment is about living from authenticity. When you know who you are and honor that truth, every connection you form — romantic, familial, or professional — is filtered through integrity. This does not guarantee perfect harmony, but it ensures that whatever unfolds is grounded in respect and truth rather than fear or pretense. From this place, relationships become less about fixing each other and more about growing together.

Health and Vitality: Healing Through Frequency and Focus

The state of your health is not only influenced by genetics or lifestyle but also by the energetic environment you create within yourself. While nutrition, sleep, and physical activity are essential, there is another layer often overlooked: the frequencies generated by your emotions and thoughts. Every feeling you hold — gratitude, resentment, joy, fear — carries a vibrational quality that subtly impacts your body's capacity to heal and regenerate. When this inner environment is coherent, the body operates with efficiency and resilience; when it is chaotic, stress signals dominate and energy is drained.

Frequency in this context refers to the measurable patterns of energy created by the nervous system and heart. Studies on heart rate variability, for example, show that positive emotional states like appreciation or calm create harmonious rhythms in the body, which in turn improve immune function and hormonal balance. Negative states like anger or chronic worry create erratic rhythms that keep the body in fight-or-flight mode. Over time, this state of stress depletes energy reserves, disrupts digestion and sleep, and slows cellular repair. Healing begins when you intentionally shift these patterns toward harmony.

Focus plays an equally vital role. Where you direct your attention acts as a signal to the body. Constantly focusing on symptoms or what feels wrong can reinforce the stress response, keeping the body locked in survival mode. Shifting focus toward healing, even while acknowledging discomfort, begins to prime the nervous system for recovery. This is not about ignoring problems but about teaching your body that safety and repair are possible. Attention becomes a tool for signaling the body to move out of defense and into restoration.

Creating an inner state conducive to healing does not mean suppressing difficult emotions. Avoidance can backfire, leading to tension and unresolved stress. Instead, the goal is emotional regulation — allowing feelings to move through you without becoming trapped in them. Simple practices like deep breathing, guided visualization, or mindful movement help recalibrate the nervous system and bring attention back to the present moment. These techniques do not heal in isolation but create the conditions in which the body's innate healing mechanisms can operate effectively.

Another important aspect of frequency and focus is belief. The body responds powerfully to perception. Placebo research has repeatedly demonstrated that expectation influences outcomes, even at the physiological level. If you believe recovery is possible, the body releases chemicals consistent with healing; if you believe you are beyond repair, stress pathways remain active. Cultivating belief does not mean blind optimism — it means creating a grounded trust in the body's ability to adapt and repair when given proper conditions.

Healing through frequency and focus also requires consistency. A single moment of calm or positivity can feel good, but lasting change emerges through daily alignment. Just as physical fitness builds through repetition, emotional and mental coherence strengthens through ongoing practice. Over time, these internal shifts create visible improvements in vitality — more stable energy, clearer thinking, and resilience in the face of stress.

To integrate this approach into daily life, begin by observing the quality of energy you bring into each moment. Notice the emotions that dominate your mornings, the thoughts that repeat throughout your day, and how your body responds to them. Awareness itself is transformative because it interrupts automatic patterns and offers space for choice. Instead of unconsciously feeding stress, you can redirect toward states that support healing — calm, gratitude, curiosity, or even quiet acceptance of where you are now.

Rituals help anchor these shifts. Setting aside a few minutes each morning to center yourself before the day begins can change the trajectory of your entire experience. This might involve breathwork, meditation, or simply sitting quietly and visualizing the kind of energy you want to carry into the day. By priming your nervous system for coherence, you prepare the body to navigate challenges without defaulting to stress responses that disrupt healing.

Movement can also be used to reinforce frequency alignment. Physical activity is not only about building strength or stamina; it is one of the fastest ways to reset the nervous system and discharge stagnant energy. Practices like walking, yoga, or stretching become more than exercise when approached with mindful presence. As you move, focus on releasing tension rather than pushing through it. This transforms movement into a dialogue with the body rather than a demand upon it.

Nutrition and environment further influence frequency. Whole, unprocessed foods support stable energy and reduce the inflammatory responses that exacerbate stress. Likewise, the spaces you inhabit — your home, workplace, or nature — shape your internal state. Surrounding yourself with order, natural light, or calming sounds creates an energetic backdrop that supports rather than hinders healing. This is not about perfection but about reducing unnecessary stress signals so your body can prioritize repair.

Another dimension of healing through frequency and focus is learning to trust subtle feedback. The body constantly communicates through sensations, energy shifts, and mood changes, but many people are conditioned to ignore these cues. By paying attention — noticing when tension eases after a deep breath, or when calm arises after a supportive thought — you strengthen the connection between mind and body. This feedback loop becomes a guide for refining practices and deepening alignment over time.

The long-term result of this work is resilience. Healing is rarely a straight line; life will still bring challenges, but your capacity to recover improves dramatically. Instead of spiraling into fear or depletion, you can return to balance more quickly. Resilience does not mean avoiding difficulty but moving through it with steadiness, knowing you have tools to recalibrate your inner state regardless of external circumstances.

Ultimately, cultivating health and vitality through frequency and focus is about creating conditions where your body's natural intelligence can do what it is designed to do: heal, adapt, and thrive. By consistently choosing thoughts, emotions, and actions that support harmony rather than chaos, you shift from surviving to living with renewed energy and presence. This transformation is subtle at first but becomes undeniable as vitality builds from the inside out.

Part IV. Embodiment and Integration

By the time you arrive at this stage, you will have explored the mechanics of hidden reality, uncovered the inner patterns shaping your experience, and practiced aligning thought, emotion, and action. But knowledge alone does not transform a life. Transformation happens when insight becomes embodiment — when the principles you have learned are no longer something you remember to apply but something you live instinctively.

Integration is where real change stabilizes. It is one thing to feel aligned during moments of meditation or reflection; it is another to maintain that alignment in the middle of ordinary life — during challenging conversations, financial decisions, or unexpected setbacks. This final part of the journey is about carrying your new awareness into every situation, so that your outer world begins to reflect the inner shifts you have cultivated.

Embodiment is not perfection. It does not mean you will never feel fear, doubt, or frustration again. Rather, it means those states no longer define you or dictate your choices. You begin to move through challenges with steadiness, recognizing them as temporary fluctuations rather than permanent barriers. This ability to stay grounded in your deeper truth, even in chaos, is what allows transformation to endure beyond the page of a book or the quiet of personal practice.

This section also focuses on the ripple effect of personal alignment. As you embody these principles, the impact naturally extends to your relationships, your work, and the environments you inhabit. People respond differently to you, opportunities seem to appear more organically, and even obstacles become opportunities for refinement rather than reasons to quit. Integration turns personal growth from an isolated pursuit into a way of living that continually evolves and expands.

What follows will help you anchor this shift. You will learn to recognize the subtle signs that confirm your movement into a higher reality, sustain alignment when life tests your progress, and redefine what it means to live beyond the ordinary. This is not about adding more techniques but about simplifying — distilling everything you have learned into daily rhythms and perspectives that feel natural and sustainable.

Part IV marks the point where transformation stops being something you chase and becomes something you are. It is the bridge between understanding and living, between glimpsing what is possible and making it your normal. This is where the work becomes effortless, not because challenges disappear, but because you have finally become the kind of person who knows how to meet them.

Chapter 10: Daily Practices That Reshape Reality

The Morning Calibration: A 15-Minute Ritual to Set Frequency

The way you begin your day sets the tone for everything that follows. Before emails, obligations, and external noise pull your focus outward, there is a window of time where your mind is impressionable and your nervous system is highly receptive. In these first minutes after waking, you are closer to subconscious states, which means any pattern you reinforce will carry through the rest of the day. This is why starting with intentional calibration — aligning your frequency and focus — is so powerful.

A morning calibration ritual does not need to be elaborate. In fact, simplicity makes it sustainable. The purpose is to shift from reactive to deliberate, from scattered to centered. In just fifteen minutes, you can prime your body and mind to operate from coherence rather than chaos, which directly influences how you interpret events, interact with others, and make decisions throughout the day.

The first component of calibration is presence. Upon waking, avoid reaching immediately for your phone or diving into tasks. Instead, sit upright, close your eyes, and breathe deeply. Pay attention to the weight of your body, the rhythm of your inhale and exhale, and the sensation of waking life moving through you. Even two or three minutes of this awareness grounds you, signaling to your nervous system that you are safe and steady. This pause creates space before the mind begins replaying yesterday's worries or anticipating today's challenges.

Once presence is established, the next step is to intentionally choose your frequency for the day. This is not about forcing yourself to feel positive but about consciously orienting toward the emotional state you want to embody — calm, gratitude, focus, or openness. You can begin by recalling a memory that evokes this state naturally, such as a moment of connection, accomplishment, or peace. Allow the associated feeling to fill your body rather than remaining abstract in your mind. When the emotion is felt physically — warmth in the chest, lightness in the breath — it becomes easier to maintain later.

From here, introduce focus. Direct your attention toward what matters most today, not as a to-do list but as an intention. Ask yourself: "What energy do I want to bring into my interactions? What outcome would feel meaningful by the end of the day?" This transforms the day from a series of tasks into an expression of your chosen state of being. The clarity this creates helps filter distractions and align choices with your deeper goals rather than fleeting impulses.

To reinforce this alignment, incorporate a brief visualization. Picture yourself moving through the day embodying the frequency you just cultivated. See yourself responding calmly to challenges, speaking with clarity, and maintaining presence even amid noise or stress. This mental rehearsal primes your subconscious, making it more likely that you will act in accordance with this vision when situations arise. The visualization is not about controlling every detail but about setting the energetic tone that will guide your actions.

Anchoring this state requires bringing it from thought into the body. A few minutes of intentional movement can bridge that gap. Gentle stretches, slow yoga postures, or even standing with feet grounded and arms raised in expansion tell the nervous system that energy is flowing and available. This physical cue enhances mental clarity and prepares you to meet the day not from tension but from openness. Movement does not need to be complex; what matters is awareness as you do it.

Integrating gratitude at this stage deepens the calibration. Gratitude is one of the most efficient ways to shift frequency because it directs attention toward sufficiency rather than lack. Take a few breaths and reflect on three things you appreciate in this moment — not grand achievements but simple realities, such as the safety of the space you are in, the strength of your body, or the opportunities present in a new day. Let yourself feel the relief and steadiness that gratitude creates, noticing how it softens mental noise and expands perspective.

After cultivating gratitude, focus briefly on alignment between intention and action. Quietly remind yourself of the choices that support the state you want to maintain. If calm is your chosen frequency, consider how you will pace your responses rather than react impulsively. If focus is your goal, identify where you will direct your energy first instead of scattering it across endless tasks. This step transforms the ritual from inspiration into practical guidance, ensuring the clarity you build in the morning carries forward into behavior.

To complete the ritual, end with stillness. Sit for a final minute with eyes closed, breathing slowly and observing the settled energy you have created. Rather than rushing into the next activity, allow this pause to mark the transition from inner preparation to outer engagement. The mind remembers endings strongly; finishing in stillness reinforces the sense of grounded presence you want to carry with you.

The entire process takes fifteen minutes, yet its effects extend far beyond that window. By calibrating first thing in the morning, you prevent the day from being dictated by external chaos. Instead, you begin with inner coherence, which subtly influences every interaction and decision. Challenges will still arise, but you meet them differently — less reactive, more centered, and better able to return to equilibrium after disruptions. Over time, this practice shifts not only how your days unfold but also how you perceive your life as a whole.

Consistency is what transforms this from a useful technique into a powerful tool. The first few mornings may feel unfamiliar, especially if you are used to rushing or starting the day in distraction. But repetition rewires patterns, and soon this ritual becomes an anchor — a signal to your mind and body that you are choosing alignment rather than defaulting to stress. This daily decision compounds, steadily reshaping both internal state and external outcomes in ways that become unmistakable.

When you begin each day by setting frequency and focus deliberately, you are no longer waiting for circumstances to dictate your experience. You step into the role of participant rather than bystander in your own life. This is how alignment moves from concept to lived reality — one intentional morning at a time.

Evening Integration: Closing the Loop of Each Day

How you close your day is as important as how you begin it. The mind and body do not simply switch off when you fall asleep; they process, integrate, and imprint everything you experienced while awake. The final thoughts and emotional states you carry into rest influence the quality of your sleep, the way your nervous system recovers overnight, and even the energy you wake up with the next morning. Evening integration ensures you end the day in coherence rather than chaos, turning sleep into a period of renewal rather than unresolved tension.

Most people finish their day in a state of mental overflow. Screens, unfinished tasks, and lingering worries create an internal restlessness that continues long after the body lies down. This disrupts natural recovery and contributes to the cycle of waking up already depleted. By intentionally closing the loop each evening, you release accumulated stress, harvest insights from the day, and align yourself with the state you want to carry into tomorrow.

The first step in evening integration is decompression. Before reflecting or planning, allow your body and mind to shift out of activity mode. This transition is easiest when you step away from stimulating inputs. Silence notifications, dim harsh lighting, and choose an environment that signals closure rather than continuation of the day's demands. A few minutes of slow breathing or gentle stretching can help the body unwind, lowering cortisol and preparing the nervous system for deeper rest.

Once decompression begins, reflection follows naturally. Review the day not as a critic but as an observer. Acknowledge moments that felt aligned — where your thoughts, emotions, and actions supported your deeper intentions — and also notice where you felt pulled off course. This is not about judgment but about awareness. By seeing patterns clearly, you prepare to adjust them without shame or defensiveness. Over time, this nightly reflection becomes a subtle recalibration, allowing each day to inform the next without carrying forward unnecessary tension.

Gratitude is central to this process. Just as in the morning, gratitude shifts the frequency of your mind and body, but in the evening it serves a unique role: it softens lingering stress and signals completion. Reflect on what you appreciate about the day, even if it was challenging. Gratitude does not require perfection; it simply requires noticing what was good, however small. This might be a kind word from someone, a moment of progress, or simply the strength to have faced what was difficult. Allowing yourself to feel gratitude before rest reorients your subconscious toward sufficiency rather than lack.

The evening ritual is also an opportunity to release what no longer needs to be carried. Unfinished tasks, emotional friction, and unresolved questions can weigh heavily on the nervous system if left unacknowledged. Writing them down — either as a simple list or as free-form journaling — creates psychological closure. By externalizing thoughts, you free the mind from cycling through them while you sleep. This is especially effective when paired with an intentional statement such as, "I release this for now; I will return to it with clarity tomorrow."

Releasing the day also involves letting go of emotional residue. Conflicts, regrets, or moments of self-criticism can linger in the body as unprocessed tension. Rather than suppressing these feelings or carrying them forward, acknowledge them directly. Name the emotion — frustration, sadness, worry — and allow yourself to feel it without judgment. Then guide yourself toward closure by asking, "What do I need to forgive, either in myself or in others, so that I can rest fully tonight?" Forgiveness here is not about excusing behavior but about unburdening yourself so healing can continue while you sleep.

A brief visualization can deepen this sense of completion. Imagine a mental container or a symbolic space — a journal, a box, or even a light-filled room — where the events of the day are stored safely. Picture yourself placing each thought or unresolved matter there, trusting that it will be available for review tomorrow if needed. This practice reassures the mind that nothing important will be lost while also granting permission to rest without constant vigilance.

The next step is intentional focus on the state you want to carry into sleep. As you lie down or sit quietly, choose a frequency such as peace, gratitude, or renewal. Breathe deeply and imagine this feeling expanding through your body, softening muscles, slowing your heartbeat, and quieting mental noise. Sleep entered from this state tends to be more restorative, as the nervous system remains in balance rather than cycling through stress responses. Over time, this pattern conditions the body to associate nighttime with healing rather than tension.

Integration also means harvesting insights from the day's experiences. After reflection and release, consider what lessons or truths emerged. This is not about overanalyzing every detail but about noticing subtle shifts in perspective: Did you respond differently to a familiar trigger? Did you recognize a new boundary or value? By acknowledging even small growth, you reinforce progress and prepare to carry it forward. These nightly recognitions become stepping stones for continuous transformation rather than isolated moments of awareness.

Closing the loop of the day can also include a quiet setting of intention for tomorrow. Rather than listing tasks, choose a guiding principle: presence, patience, courage, or focus. Allow this word or phrase to settle into your mind as you prepare for rest. It serves as a soft anchor that bridges one day to the next, ensuring continuity without burdening the mind with excessive planning.

The ritual ends in stillness, allowing your body to register the shift from doing to being. Sit or lie quietly for a minute or two, focusing on your breath and the calm that has replaced the day's momentum. This final moment is powerful because it creates a distinct threshold between waking activity and restorative rest. Over time, the body learns to anticipate this rhythm, making it easier to transition into sleep and wake with greater clarity and energy.

When practiced consistently, evening integration becomes more than a nightly routine; it becomes a form of self-respect. It signals that your experiences matter enough to process, your growth matters enough to acknowledge, and your rest matters enough to protect. This quiet closing of the day turns sleep into an ally for transformation rather than a pause between cycles of stress, allowing you to live each day with more intention and alignment than the one before.

Micro-Practices for In-the-Moment Alignment (Anytime, Anywhere)

Big breakthroughs often begin with small choices. While dedicated morning and evening rituals create powerful anchors, life is full of moments where alignment slips — in a tense conversation, during unexpected delays, or in the middle of work deadlines. These moments determine whether you remain centered or spiral into old patterns. Micro-practices are the bridge between structured rituals and real-life application. They are quick, adaptable techniques that help you reset frequency and focus in seconds, no matter where you are.

The power of micro-practices lies in their simplicity. They do not require a quiet room, special equipment, or even much time. Their effectiveness comes from interrupting automatic reactions and reconnecting you to presence. When practiced consistently, these short resets create a cumulative effect. You spend less time lost in reactivity and more time responding from clarity. Over weeks and months, this becomes a subtle yet profound shift in how you navigate your entire life.

One of the most fundamental micro-practices is the single conscious breath. When tension spikes, deliberately pause and take one slow, deep inhale, followed by an equally slow exhale. Focus fully on the sensation of air moving in and out, allowing everything else to fade for that moment. This simple act signals safety to the nervous system, interrupting the stress response and opening space for intentional choice rather than unconscious reaction. It may only take five seconds, yet it can transform how you handle the next five minutes.

Another powerful technique is the sensory check-in. This involves grounding yourself through immediate physical awareness: noticing what you see, hear, touch, or smell in the present moment. For example, feel your feet against the floor, notice the temperature of the air, or observe subtle background sounds. By anchoring attention to sensory input, you shift out of mental rumination and into embodied presence. This practice is particularly useful during high-stress environments where mental loops can easily take over.

Micro-practices can also involve subtle reframing of thoughts. When you catch yourself in a spiral of negativity or fear, ask a grounding question such as, "What is actually true right now?" or "What else could this mean?" This interrupts distorted narratives and creates a space for perspective. Even if circumstances do not change, your relationship to them softens, allowing more constructive action. Over time, this reframing builds resilience by training your mind to question automatic assumptions rather than blindly follow them.

Small physical gestures can serve as alignment triggers as well. Placing your hand on your heart, rolling your shoulders back, or standing tall with both feet grounded are all ways to signal safety and confidence to the body. These movements may seem minor, but the body's posture and the mind's state are deeply linked. When the body shifts toward openness and balance, the mind follows. Such gestures are subtle enough to use in public without drawing attention, making them accessible in any setting.

These practices do not replace deeper inner work; they complement it. By weaving them into your daily life, you create a network of small alignment points that prevent minor stressors from accumulating into major disconnection. Instead of waiting for the next morning or evening ritual to reset, you carry tools with you everywhere — ready to return to coherence at a moment's notice.

Another effective micro-practice is the silent affirmation. This is not about repeating empty phrases but choosing a statement that aligns with your current intention and grounding it in the body. For example, silently saying "I am safe," "I am capable," or "I choose calm" while pairing the words with a slow breath links thought and physiology. Over time, these statements become cues for the nervous system to downshift into stability. The key is consistency; using the same phrase repeatedly strengthens its impact, turning it into a conditioned signal of alignment.

Mini visualizations also work well when you need a rapid reset. In moments of overwhelm, imagine stepping back from the situation as if viewing it from above. This mental distance helps soften emotional intensity and brings clarity. Alternatively, picture a calming image — sunlight filtering through trees, waves rolling on a shore, or light expanding from your chest — and let your body respond to the imagined peace. The mind does not distinguish strongly between vividly imagined experiences and real ones, which makes this a powerful tool for immediate regulation.

Short gratitude scans can transform mood in seconds. Simply pause and identify one thing in your immediate environment you appreciate. It could be the comfort of your chair, the support of someone nearby, or even the chance to breathe and recalibrate. This small act redirects attention away from what is lacking toward what is present, interrupting stress and reorienting the nervous system toward sufficiency. Gratitude practiced this way becomes less about lists and more about lived awareness, something you can return to repeatedly throughout the day.

One overlooked but powerful alignment tool is micro-pausing before transitions. Every time you shift from one activity to another — leaving a meeting, opening an email, walking into a room — take one intentional breath before proceeding. These pauses prevent accumulated stress from carrying over into the next moment. They also create a sense of rhythm in your day, replacing constant forward momentum with moments of integration. This habit alone can significantly reduce exhaustion and help you maintain presence across changing circumstances.

Touch points in your physical environment can serve as cues for alignment. For example, each time you pass through a doorway or sit down at your desk, use it as a signal to check your posture, breathe deeply, or recall your chosen frequency for the day. These environmental anchors turn ordinary moments into opportunities for coherence. Over time, they form a web of subtle reminders woven throughout your routines, ensuring alignment is never far from reach.

The effectiveness of these micro-practices is not measured by their complexity but by their repetition and sincerity. A single conscious breath will not transform your life on its own, but hundreds of such breaths taken over weeks and months will recondition your baseline state. You spend more time in calm focus and less time recovering from disconnection. This is how incremental shifts compound into meaningful transformation.

Ultimately, these practices cultivate a life where alignment is not something reserved for quiet mornings or special rituals but a thread woven through every moment. The more you use them, the less you feel at the mercy of external circumstances and the more you realize you can return to presence at any time. That sense of inner steadiness, available in an instant, is one of the most valuable skills you can develop — and it becomes the foundation for living in continuous connection with the deeper reality you are learning to access.

Chapter 11: Living Permanently in the "Secret Side"

Signs You've Shifted Into a Higher Reality

When inner alignment begins to take root, life starts reflecting it back in subtle but unmistakable ways. These changes are not always dramatic at first. They often emerge quietly — a shift in perception, an unexpected ease in situations that once felt heavy, a series of coincidences that seem too precise to dismiss. Recognizing these signs is essential because they confirm that the work you have done internally is translating into real transformation. Without this awareness, you might overlook progress or assume nothing is changing simply because external results have not yet fully materialized.

The first sign is a noticeable shift in how you experience challenges. Difficulties may still arise, but your relationship to them changes. Instead of immediately slipping into panic or resistance, you find a capacity to pause, observe, and respond more intentionally. This does not mean you feel calm every moment, but there is a baseline steadiness beneath the waves. Problems that once triggered spirals of fear or self-doubt begin to feel like opportunities for growth rather than threats to your security. This subtle resilience is one of the clearest indicators of higher alignment.

Another sign is the increasing frequency of synchronicities. These are moments when life seems to organize itself around your intentions without forced effort — you think of someone and they call, you stumble upon exactly the resource you need at the right time, or a series of small events align perfectly to open a new path. While synchronicities can occur randomly, when they become regular and consistent, they signal that your inner state and outer reality are resonating more harmoniously.

A heightened sense of clarity also begins to emerge. This clarity is less about having every answer and more about knowing which direction feels aligned. Decisions that once caused confusion begin to feel more obvious. You may notice a stronger intuition — subtle gut feelings or quiet inner nudges that guide you toward choices that ultimately prove beneficial. Trusting these impressions becomes easier because you see evidence that following them leads to better outcomes.

Your emotional baseline shifts as well. Joy, peace, or gratitude may arise more spontaneously, without needing specific reasons. These feelings are not constant, but they become more accessible, appearing even in ordinary moments like drinking coffee, walking outside, or talking with a friend. This growing ability to feel contentment without external validation is a hallmark of higher alignment — it shows that your sense of well-being is rooted within rather than dependent on circumstances.

Another indicator is a change in what you tolerate. Misaligned relationships, environments, or habits that once felt normal begin to feel heavy or out of place. You may find yourself naturally drawn to healthier patterns and less willing to engage in dynamics that drain you. This shift does not arise from force or judgment; it happens organically as your internal frequency no longer resonates with lower patterns. In many ways, you outgrow them quietly rather than battling them directly.

You may also notice a different sense of timing. Life begins to feel less like a constant race and more like a flow you are learning to trust. The pressure to control every outcome lessens as you observe how things often unfold at the right moment without your interference. Patience develops naturally, not as forced restraint but as a deeper knowing that alignment draws the right opportunities when you are ready to receive them. This shift in timing is subtle yet powerful; it transforms anxiety about the future into quiet anticipation.

Relationships reflect this transformation as well. People who resonate with your new state may begin entering your life unexpectedly, while others who no longer align may naturally drift away. Conversations take on more depth, and connections that once felt strained may soften as your energy changes. You become less reactive to others' triggers and more grounded in your own presence, which can invite others to meet you at that same level of authenticity. This does not mean every relationship becomes effortless, but you notice more harmony in interactions and a stronger ability to navigate conflict without losing your center.

Your perception of the world itself begins to shift. Colors may appear more vivid, small details stand out, and moments of beauty seem to present themselves with greater frequency. Ordinary experiences — a breeze through a window, the sound of laughter, the warmth of sunlight — evoke genuine appreciation. This heightened awareness is not about seeking constant euphoria but about recognizing richness in the everyday. It signals that your attention is no longer clouded by constant worry or projection, allowing you to fully inhabit the present.

Another sign of higher alignment is the quiet dissolution of old compulsions. Habits driven by fear, scarcity, or the need for external approval lose their grip as you become more anchored in self-trust. This can manifest as reduced urgency to overwork, a shift away from unhealthy coping mechanisms, or a new ease in saying no without guilt. Change in this area often happens gradually, yet the cumulative effect is profound: your life feels lighter because it is no longer shaped by constant resistance or self-betrayal.

There is also an increased sense of interconnectedness. You begin to notice how your internal state influences not just your personal experience but the environment around you. A calm presence soothes tense situations; gratitude attracts cooperation; authenticity inspires openness. This awareness deepens responsibility without burden — you recognize that your alignment is not only for your benefit but also impacts those you encounter. This perspective fosters compassion and motivates you to maintain alignment not as a private pursuit but as a way of contributing to a wider ripple of change.

The clearest confirmation of this shift is the quiet confidence that grows within you. It is not loud or performative but steady and grounded. You feel less need to prove yourself or seek validation because your sense of worth no longer hinges on external conditions. This internal assurance allows you to move through uncertainty with trust and to meet challenges without collapsing into self-doubt. Over time, this becomes one of the most valuable outcomes of higher alignment — a way of living anchored in deep, unshakable stability.

Maintaining Alignment in Chaos or Crisis

True alignment is tested not during moments of ease but in the middle of chaos. It is one thing to remain centered when life flows smoothly and another to hold that center when uncertainty, conflict, or loss arrives without warning. Crisis compresses time and amplifies emotions, pulling old fears and patterns to the surface. In these moments, your ability to stay connected to the deeper principles you have cultivated determines whether you spiral into reactivity or navigate with grounded clarity.

The first step in maintaining alignment during chaos is recognizing the physiological impact of stress. In moments of crisis, the body floods with adrenaline and cortisol, priming you for fight, flight, or freeze. Awareness of this response is crucial because it allows you to separate the biochemical surge from the actual circumstances. Instead of mistaking the body's reaction for the truth of the situation, you can acknowledge, "This is my nervous system responding," and begin calming it before making decisions. Simple grounding techniques — deep breathing, feeling your feet on the floor, or placing a hand on your chest — send immediate signals of safety, creating space to respond rather than react.

Equally important is controlling where your focus goes. Chaos tempts the mind to fixate on worst-case scenarios or on every detail outside your control. This fragmented attention intensifies fear and diminishes your ability to act effectively. Reclaiming focus begins by asking one grounding question: "What is within my influence right now?" Redirecting attention to actionable steps — even something as simple as slowing your breath or making a single phone call — interrupts spiraling and restores a sense of agency.

Maintaining alignment also involves remembering your why. In the midst of crisis, perspective narrows; survival instincts override deeper values. Reconnecting to what matters most — your core commitments, relationships, or guiding principles — serves as a stabilizing force. It prevents decisions made from fear alone and ensures that your actions align with who you want to be, not just what you are trying to avoid. This connection to purpose often provides strength that adrenaline cannot.

It is equally vital to allow emotions without being consumed by them. Suppressing fear, grief, or anger does not create alignment; it drives them underground, where they resurface in destructive ways. The key is to witness emotions as passing waves rather than permanent states. Naming what you feel ("This is fear," "This is grief") creates enough distance to process without judgment. Paradoxically, this gentle acknowledgment often softens the intensity and allows clarity to emerge more quickly.

Another strategy is to simplify in moments of chaos. Complexity overwhelms an already taxed nervous system, leading to confusion and paralysis. Simplifying means prioritizing what truly matters and releasing what does not require immediate attention. It may involve narrowing your focus to the next right action rather than attempting to solve everything at once. This step-by-step approach prevents collapse under the weight of the entire situation and builds momentum toward resolution.

Staying aligned also requires conscious management of input. During chaos, the environment often amplifies fear through constant news updates, conflicting opinions, or the emotional states of those around you. While staying informed is important, overexposure drains focus and reinforces anxiety. Creating intentional boundaries around information — limiting how often you check updates, choosing reliable sources, and stepping away when your nervous system feels saturated — preserves mental clarity. Equally important is seeking environments and conversations that steady you rather than escalate panic.

Support networks become especially valuable during these times. Alignment does not mean handling everything alone; it means discerning who can provide grounded presence rather than fuel chaos. This might be a trusted friend, mentor, or even a quiet space in nature that feels stabilizing. Allowing yourself to lean on external support is not weakness but wisdom — it acknowledges that resilience is strengthened through connection, not isolation.

Reflection after immediate turbulence is another key element. Once the situation stabilizes even slightly, take time to review how you navigated it. Notice where you stayed aligned and where you were pulled off center. This is not for self-criticism but for refinement. Each crisis, no matter how disruptive, offers insight into your triggers and strengths. Over time, this reflective practice builds a kind of internal map, making future storms less disorienting because you recognize the terrain.

A profound shift occurs when you begin to view chaos not as something to eliminate but as an invitation to deepen alignment. While the instinct to seek control is strong, real stability comes from flexibility — the ability to adapt without losing your center. This mindset turns crisis into a proving ground for the principles you have cultivated, revealing how deeply they have been integrated. Rather than asking, "How can I avoid chaos?" the question becomes, "Who do I choose to be within it?"

Practical anchors help maintain this perspective. Short breathing exercises, brief pauses before responding, and grounding phrases can be inserted directly into challenging moments. For example, silently repeating "I can meet this one moment" or "I choose calm now" disrupts the escalation of fear and brings focus to the present step instead of the overwhelming totality of the crisis. These micro-interventions may seem small, but layered together they create a stable thread of alignment even in turbulent conditions.

In the aftermath of chaos, integration matters as much as survival. Unprocessed stress lingers in the body and can erode alignment long after the immediate crisis passes. Taking time to rest, release tension, and reflect ensures the experience strengthens you rather than hardens you. This might involve journaling, intentional movement, or quiet time in nature to allow the nervous system to recalibrate. Healing from chaos is not indulgent; it is the foundation that allows you to meet future challenges with greater steadiness and clarity.

The ultimate sign of maintaining alignment is recognizing that chaos no longer defines you. Circumstances may be unpredictable, but your identity and direction remain anchored. This does not remove discomfort, but it does prevent you from being swept entirely into fear or despair. Over time, you come to trust that even in crisis, the deeper reality you have connected to is still present — guiding, sustaining, and waiting to be re-accessed as soon as you remember to return to it.

The Path Forward: Building a Life Beyond the Ordinary

Crossing the threshold into higher alignment is not the end of the journey. It is the point where living differently becomes possible. The shift you have cultivated internally begins to influence every choice, relationship, and action. What follows is the work of building a life that reflects this new state — a life that is not just about avoiding struggle but about actively creating meaning, depth, and fulfillment.

Living beyond the ordinary starts with redefining what ordinary even means. For many, ordinary has been shaped by patterns of reaction: working without purpose, chasing external validation, and measuring success by comparison. As alignment deepens, those measures lose their appeal. The focus shifts from what looks impressive to others to what feels deeply congruent to you. This requires honesty about what you value most and the courage to align daily decisions with those values, even when it challenges expectations around you.

One of the first changes you will notice is how intention replaces autopilot. Rather than being carried along by default routines or external pressures, you begin choosing deliberately — how you spend your time, what energy you bring into interactions, and which opportunities you pursue. This level of choice can feel unfamiliar at first because it requires active participation rather than passivity. Yet this is precisely what makes it powerful: alignment stops being something you visit during quiet moments and becomes something you inhabit continuously.

Building a life beyond the ordinary also demands integration across all areas, not just personal growth practices. Work, relationships, health, and even leisure begin to reflect your deeper principles. This does not mean everything changes overnight, but you start noticing where there is harmony and where there is friction. In places where alignment is absent, you are less willing to settle. That unwillingness is not restlessness; it is clarity. It signals that your internal shift is becoming external.

There is also a growing awareness of contribution. As you stabilize in alignment, your attention naturally expands beyond personal gain to include the impact you have on others. Fulfillment begins to come not just from achieving goals but from knowing your presence uplifts the environments you inhabit. This is not about sacrificing yourself; it is about recognizing that alignment radiates outward and creates opportunities for collective growth. In many ways, the path forward becomes less about seeking extraordinary events and more about embodying extraordinary presence in everyday life.

This stage of the journey is both liberating and challenging. It liberates you from old constraints, but it also requires ongoing vigilance to remain true to what you have discovered. Alignment is dynamic, not static; life will continue to test it through change and uncertainty. The question is no longer whether you know the principles but whether you will keep living them when circumstances fluctuate. Building a life beyond the ordinary means accepting this as lifelong practice rather than a single transformation.

Sustaining this level of living requires a willingness to continually recalibrate. Alignment is not a single choice but a series of choices made day after day. There will be times when old habits resurface, when external pressures tempt you back into patterns that once felt safe. These moments are not failures but invitations to recommit. By noticing them without judgment, you gain the ability to course-correct more quickly, shortening the gap between slipping out of alignment and returning to it.

An important part of this process is learning to recognize subtle signals that guide your next steps. Intuition often speaks softly, through quiet impressions rather than loud commands. As you trust and act on these impressions, life tends to respond with confirmation — small openings, coincidences, or a sense of ease that affirms you are on the right track. This feedback loop deepens self-trust and reduces reliance on constant external validation.

Creating a life beyond the ordinary also involves embracing periods of discomfort. Growth often requires letting go of what is familiar even when it no longer fits. Relationships may shift, priorities may realign, and parts of your identity may dissolve as new ones emerge. These transitions can feel unsettling, yet they are evidence that transformation is occurring at a deep level. Rather than resisting discomfort, you learn to hold it with patience, understanding that every expansion requires space to unfold.

Over time, fulfillment arises less from achieving milestones and more from the quality of presence you bring to each moment. You begin to notice that life feels richer not because everything is perfect but because you are fully engaged with it. Ordinary experiences — a meal with loved ones, a walk outside, even completing a simple task — take on depth when approached with alignment. This shift reframes success itself, moving it from something pursued in the future to something cultivated now.

As you continue, contribution naturally integrates into your path. The energy you carry influences more than your personal reality; it impacts every interaction and environment you touch. People sense it in the steadiness of your presence, in the authenticity of your words, and in the quiet confidence that comes from living aligned. Without forcing it, you become an example for others, showing that transformation is not about escaping life but about engaging it fully and consciously.

Ultimately, building a life beyond the ordinary is not about perfection but integration. It is about weaving the principles you have learned into the fabric of everyday living until they become second nature. You will still encounter challenges and moments of doubt, but your baseline shifts. Instead of constantly seeking alignment, you begin living from it. In this way, the extraordinary is no longer something you chase; it is the foundation from which you create.

Conclusion: The New Map of Reality

Integrating the Framework Into Everyday Life

Understanding the principles behind alignment is only the first step. Real transformation happens when those principles stop being separate from daily life and start shaping how you approach ordinary moments. Integration is about closing the gap between insight and habit. It is the difference between knowing what creates change and living as someone for whom change has already occurred.

Most people treat personal growth as something they visit rather than inhabit — a meditation here, a workshop there, brief glimpses of clarity followed by a return to old patterns. True integration reverses this dynamic. The practices and perspectives you have learned become woven into the fabric of your day, so alignment is no longer an event but a way of being. This shift may sound subtle, yet it determines whether the changes you have experienced endure or fade under the weight of routine.

The first step toward integration is to recognize that small moments carry as much power as major ones. Waiting in traffic, responding to a stressful email, or making a simple choice about how to spend your evening all become opportunities to align thought, emotion, and action. These moments might seem insignificant, but they are where habits are formed and reinforced. Each choice conditions your nervous system and trains your mind toward either coherence or fragmentation. When you treat daily decisions as practice grounds for alignment, growth accelerates naturally.

Consistency is more important than intensity. A single profound breakthrough can feel life-changing, but its impact fades without repeated application. Conversely, quiet daily choices — choosing presence in a conversation, taking one conscious breath before reacting, returning to gratitude before sleep — compound over time. Integration happens in this accumulation. The power lies not in occasional dramatic effort but in steady, repeated alignment that becomes instinctive.

Living from this framework also involves embracing imperfection. There will be days when you forget, when you react impulsively, when fear or old patterns resurface. Integration does not mean eliminating these moments but learning to meet them differently. Instead of spiraling into self-criticism, you acknowledge the slip, realign, and move forward. This compassionate approach prevents growth from becoming another arena for perfectionism and keeps the process sustainable over the long term.

A practical way to support integration is to create subtle anchors throughout your environment. These are gentle reminders that prompt alignment without demanding conscious effort. It might be a phrase on a notecard at your desk, a mindful pause each time you open a door, or a short reflection before meals. These cues link ordinary actions to deeper awareness, training your nervous system to associate alignment with daily rhythms rather than isolated practices.

The key is not to add more complexity but to simplify. Integration succeeds when the principles you have learned feel natural, not forced. Instead of overhauling your schedule or striving for constant vigilance, begin with the smallest, most repeatable actions. Over time, these accumulate into a quiet but undeniable shift: alignment becomes less about what you do and more about who you are becoming.

Another important layer of integration is understanding that alignment is dynamic rather than fixed. Your frequency, focus, and emotional state will naturally fluctuate throughout the day. Instead of expecting uninterrupted steadiness, aim for the ability to return to center more quickly. This skill grows through repetition; each time you notice misalignment and gently recalibrate, you reinforce the neural pathways that make alignment easier to access next time. Over weeks and months, this responsiveness becomes second nature.

Integration also deepens when reflection is built into your daily rhythm. Taking a few minutes at the end of the day to review how you showed up — where you felt connected, where you felt reactive, and what you learned — transforms experiences into wisdom. This quiet review is not about dwelling on mistakes but about harvesting insight. When done consistently, it creates a feedback loop that accelerates growth because every day informs the next.

The framework becomes even more powerful when shared with others. Alignment naturally radiates outward, and when you embody it consistently, people notice. Without lecturing or persuading, your presence alone can invite others into greater awareness. Conversations shift, relationships deepen, and environments become calmer simply because you are carrying coherence within you. This does not mean trying to fix others; it means becoming an anchor so they can find their own center more easily.

One of the challenges of integration is sustaining it during periods of transition or stress. These are the moments when old habits tend to resurface. Having simple grounding practices — even a single deep breath or brief pause before responding — provides a lifeline during turbulence. These micro-adjustments may feel small in the moment, yet they prevent the return to full autopilot and preserve the alignment you have worked hard to cultivate.

Over time, integration begins to shift your identity. You stop seeing yourself as someone trying to improve and start recognizing yourself as someone who lives differently. Choices that once felt forced become effortless because they align with who you now are. This identity-level change is what makes the transformation lasting. When alignment is part of your self-concept, it does not require constant willpower; it flows naturally from how you see yourself.

Perhaps the most profound outcome of integration is the quiet confidence it brings. Life still contains uncertainty, but your relationship to it changes. Instead of feeling at the mercy of circumstances, you recognize your ability to influence your experience through how you show up. This sense of agency does not eliminate difficulty, but it dissolves helplessness. You meet challenges with curiosity rather than dread, knowing that every moment offers an opportunity to practice alignment and embody the deeper truths you have uncovered.

In the end, integration is about living the teachings rather than visiting them. It is about bringing the insights you have gathered into the smallest moments of daily life until they stop feeling like practices and start feeling like your natural way of being. This is where transformation solidifies — not in occasional breakthroughs but in the steady rhythm of an aligned life, lived day after day.

The Ripple Effect: How Changing Yourself Changes Everything

Every shift you make within yourself radiates outward in ways that are often invisible at first. The world responds to who you are being, not just what you are doing. When you change your internal state, the quality of your presence changes, and this presence silently influences the people and environments around you. This is the ripple effect — transformation that begins in the unseen and moves through every layer of your life.

The first layer of the ripple is your immediate energy. Alignment alters the way you enter a room, the tone of your voice, and even the way you listen. People may not consciously understand why they feel different around you, but they sense it. A calm presence eases tension, a grounded presence inspires trust, and an authentic presence invites others to be real in return. Without needing to convince anyone of anything, you begin shifting dynamics simply by embodying coherence rather than chaos.

This influence extends to relationships. As you release old patterns of reactivity and fear, the way you interact with others transforms. Conversations become less about defending yourself or proving your worth and more about connection and understanding. The absence of defensive energy often softens the other person's posture as well. Over time, this creates healthier dynamics, not because you forced change on others, but because you modeled it.

Even when others do not change, your experience of them does. By remaining aligned, you stop being pulled into drama or cycles of blame. You recognize that their reactions are about their state, not your worth. This perspective creates freedom; you can engage with compassion without taking responsibility for fixing them. Ironically, this release of control often inspires the very shifts you once tried to force.

The ripple effect also touches opportunities and circumstances. Alignment influences not only how you perceive life but how life perceives you. When you consistently act from clarity and purpose, you attract situations that reflect those qualities. This is not about magical thinking but about resonance. People who share your values are drawn to collaborate, doors open where resistance once existed, and resources seem to arrive at the right moment. It feels like synchronicity, but it is the natural result of living congruently.

Perhaps the most surprising ripple is internal. As you transform, you begin noticing patterns you never saw before — the ways your thoughts shape your emotions, the subtle feedback your body provides, the small shifts in energy that precede major decisions. You become more sensitive to the interplay between inner and outer worlds, which allows you to adjust more skillfully. This self-awareness accelerates growth; the more you see, the more you can choose.

What begins as personal work evolves into collective impact. When one person embodies alignment, it creates permission for others to do the same. This is how cultural shifts begin — not always through grand speeches or movements, but through countless individuals choosing to live differently. Each aligned choice plants a seed, whether or not you witness its growth. Over time, these small influences accumulate into meaningful change that extends far beyond you.

The effects of this shift often reveal themselves gradually. At first, the differences may feel subtle — a lighter tone in a conversation, a moment of unexpected patience, or a decision that once felt impossible now emerging naturally. Over time, these subtleties compound, creating outcomes that look like sudden breakthroughs to those on the outside. In reality, they are the visible result of countless internal adjustments that have been taking place quietly within you.

One profound change is the way you begin influencing environments that once drained you. Places that used to feel chaotic — workplaces filled with tension, family dynamics rooted in old wounds — do not hold the same power over you. Your energy no longer feeds the cycle; instead, it offers an alternative. Without demanding anything of others, you become a steady point in the room, a quiet reminder that another way of being is possible. This alone can alter group dynamics, often without a single word.

The ripple also reshapes how you approach your goals. Rather than pursuing them from a place of lack or proving, you begin moving toward them from a foundation of sufficiency. This shift transforms the process itself. Effort becomes focused rather than frantic, decisions come from clarity rather than fear, and success is measured by alignment rather than comparison. Ironically, this mindset often leads to better results because it removes the inner resistance that once slowed you down.

As you integrate these changes, your perception of influence evolves. You recognize that true impact is not about control but resonance. Trying to convince or push others rarely works; living in alignment and allowing them to witness the results is far more persuasive. People feel authenticity more deeply than arguments, and over time, authenticity wins trust. This is why quiet transformation often creates more lasting influence than loud persuasion.

The ripple effect also prepares you to handle expansion without losing yourself. As alignment attracts opportunities and deeper connections, life may grow fuller and more complex. The same practices that helped you navigate earlier challenges — presence, emotional regulation, and clarity of intention — become essential for sustaining growth. What once felt like discipline transforms into a natural rhythm, allowing you to carry coherence into larger arenas without being consumed by them.

This influence extends beyond personal relationships or professional circles. It subtly shifts how you engage with the collective. You may feel called to contribute to causes, create work that inspires, or simply show up more fully for your community. The change is not forced; it arises naturally from an overflowing state. When you are no longer consumed by inner fragmentation, energy is freed to support something larger than yourself.

Ultimately, the ripple effect reinforces a profound truth: personal change is never truly personal. Every thought you shift, every belief you release, every moment you choose presence over reactivity sends subtle waves outward. These waves influence not only the quality of your own life but also the lives of those you may never meet. This understanding transforms personal growth from a private pursuit into a quiet act of service, demonstrating that by changing yourself, you inevitably change the world around you.

Final Invitation to Step Fully Into the Hidden Side of Reality

Reaching this point in the journey, you have uncovered layers of reality that many people never pause to examine. You have seen how thoughts, emotions, and alignment quietly shape experience; how invisible laws govern outcomes; and how transformation begins not with external conditions but with the inner state you bring to them. The principles you have explored are no longer abstract ideas but a framework you can recognize in daily life. The question now is whether you will fully step into this way of living or return to the familiar patterns of the ordinary.

Crossing this threshold is not about perfection. It is about commitment. The hidden side of reality is available to anyone willing to engage it consistently, yet few do. Most hesitate because they wait for certainty before acting — proof that alignment works, guarantees of success, or reassurance that they will not stumble along the way. That certainty never comes. The path forward requires a leap, not because the leap is reckless, but because trust cannot be built from the sidelines. It emerges only through participation.

This invitation is therefore personal. It is not a call to adopt more rules or chase constant bliss. It is a call to live with awareness — to choose alignment in small moments, to meet challenges without abandoning yourself, and to allow the quiet principles beneath reality to guide how you engage the world. This choice does not make life effortless; it makes it meaningful. It transforms every situation, not by removing difficulty, but by revealing purpose within it.

To step fully into this hidden side is to stop waiting for external validation and begin living as if what you now know is true. It means trusting that your frequency shapes experience, that inner coherence draws clarity, and that the unseen patterns you have felt pulling at the edges of your life are real. This trust does not arise overnight; it is cultivated each time you act in alignment even when fear or doubt tells you otherwise.

What makes this path powerful is its accessibility. It does not require special conditions or rare opportunities. It asks only that you bring awareness to the life you are already living. Every interaction, every choice, every quiet moment becomes part of the practice. Even setbacks and challenges serve as teachers, revealing where deeper alignment is needed. This approach removes the illusion that growth happens someday in the future; it happens here, now, in the present rhythm of your days.

The deeper invitation is to embody what you have learned rather than simply understand it. Insights held in the mind can inspire, but they only transform when lived. Embodiment means allowing these principles to inform how you speak, how you work, how you relate to others, and how you hold yourself during uncertainty. It is no longer about glimpsing alignment in isolated moments but carrying it into all corners of your life until it becomes the foundation rather than the exception.

Choosing to live this way inevitably redefines success. Rather than measuring your life solely by external milestones, you begin to evaluate it by the quality of your alignment and the integrity of your choices. Achievements and recognition may still come, but they are no longer the foundation of your sense of worth. This shift creates a quiet kind of freedom — the freedom to pursue what matters without being trapped by the need for constant approval or comparison.

Saying yes to this path also means embracing the unknown. The hidden side of reality is not about controlling every outcome but about learning to navigate uncertainty with trust. When you stop demanding that life conform to rigid expectations, you create space for possibilities you could not have planned. This is where synchronicity flourishes. By holding intentions lightly and staying receptive, you discover opportunities that often exceed what you imagined when you were trying to force results.

The work ahead is not about becoming someone entirely different but about remembering who you already are beneath the noise. Much of personal transformation is unlearning — releasing inherited beliefs, outdated scripts, and conditioned fears that obscure your natural clarity. As these layers fall away, you do not become a new person so much as you return to a truer version of yourself, one that was always present but often overlooked.

To fully step into this way of being is to commit to ongoing practice. There will be days when alignment feels effortless and days when it feels distant. Both are part of the process. What matters is the willingness to return, again and again, no matter how many times you drift. Each return strengthens the pattern until alignment becomes your baseline rather than a state you have to chase.

This path is not linear. Growth often arrives in cycles — moments of expansion followed by integration, clarity followed by challenge. Viewing these cycles as natural prevents discouragement when old patterns resurface. Each layer revisited offers an opportunity to deepen your mastery. Rather than starting over, you spiral upward, revisiting familiar themes with greater awareness and capacity each time.

Ultimately, the invitation is simple yet profound: live as though reality is responsive to your inner state, because it is. Live as though alignment matters more than appearance, because it does. Live as though your presence carries impact beyond what you can see, because it does. This perspective transforms how you meet each day. It turns ordinary interactions into opportunities to create harmony and imbues even small actions with meaning.

If you choose this path, expect your life to change quietly at first. The shifts may not be dramatic or immediately visible, but over time they accumulate. The way you experience challenges, the relationships you nurture, and the opportunities you attract begin to reflect your inner coherence. Eventually, what once felt extraordinary becomes your new normal. You realize you are no longer visiting the hidden side of reality — you are living from it.

www.ingramcontent.com/pod-product-compliance
Lightning Source LLC
Chambersburg PA
CBHW050644160426
43194CB00010B/1800